AI for Brands

Embracing the Future

Tery Spataro

Frank Sikernitsky, Whitney Tindale,

with Nelson Freitas and Sanjay Gupta

INTELLECTUAL PRESS
Imprint of Ideas
99 Wall Street
Suite 1789
New York, New York 10005

Books may be purchased in quantity and/or special sales by contacting Intellectual Press at ip@intellectualpress.com or by calling 212-498-9272

[1. Computers 2. Business]

Library of Congress Control Number: 2023921743

ISBN: 978-1-946670-11-3

10 9 8 7 6 5 4 3 2 1

Book Design by Tery Spataro
Cover Design by Tery Spataro
Illustrations by Tery Spataro

People and Brands embracing
the future with AI.

Table of Contents

AI for Brands, Embracing the Future

SKYROCKET

Foreword

Nelson Freitas, Founder, *Unknowns*

A massive thank you to Tery for inviting me to write the forward to the book – "AI for Brands: Embracing the Future'.

I'm grateful for the opportunity. "AI for Brands: Embracing the Future" demystifies and makes tangible this incredible innovation.

What is it?

Why it matters?

How AI changes our lives?

The good and the watchouts for us to consider and action on? "AI for Brands" leaves no stone unturned.

One of the bigger questions on the table is how brands will use AI. As Tery can attest I've always been passionate about brands and the vital role they play in our lives. Specifically, their ability to shape and lead culture and improve our everyday experiences. Yes – they sell things, but they do much more. For many of us, we define ourselves through our brand choices, often buying more than their products and services but adhering to their values and beliefs.

I'm sure we've all heard many of these...

> "I love Nike for what they stand for too."
>
> "I only buy Apple and don't understand those who don't."
>
> "I depend on Amazon more than I should, but they rarely mess up my order."

Regardless of how you feel about these brands, they're unwavering in what sets them apart, carry their convictions everywhere they go and rise above the rest. They're trusted and essential to many of us. AI is the new frontier for these brands and all brands –start-up to legacy - to conquer. We're curious how they will proceed – use it as a force for growth and enterprise scaling and / or a vehicle to make stand-out contributions to society and people. AI for many of us is still a blank canvas and a big unknown. In a recent Pew study, only 10% say AI helps more than it hurts. Clearly, many of us see more negatives than positives. This human anxiety is fueled by whether AI will "replace my job" and hurt my livelihood. This will inevitably become an issue for us all to deal with at a macro and societal level.

Like many of us I'm blown away by the promise of AI. It's already replacing mundane tasks in our lives and AI's future is bright in medical diagnosis and new drug therapies, the potential to make education and learning work for more of us particularly in impoverished parts of the world, innovations that will automate and techify our cars and homes, turning them into self-generating eco-systems. AI will pretty much touch every aspect of our lives – no joke. There is no escaping it. You'll will see that in "AI for Brands: Embracing the Future.

For brands, this is a pivotal moment and a fork in the road. Can they step up to ensure more of us experience AI's remarkable and profound impact?

We all know brands and companies will use AI to cut costs, scale, grow and be more efficient. All sound business choices and universal go to's. But these decisions are transactional, short-term in nature and not necessarily reputational boosting with customers and employees. At worse, if done too aggressively or widespread, set up an adversarial relationship with the people they serve.

The more human and unique opportunity is to use and embrace AI to lift and celebrate more of us. To use AI to point in a new direction that encompasses a shared belief and need. Help us be and do better – our health, well-being, education, new skills, our communities etc.

From doomsday predictions to amazing breakthroughs, the outcomes depend on us – not an external force that is beyond us. We are in control. Using AI to reinforce human disparities and insecurities is short-sighted and cruel. We can't lose sight of this.

Every brand, whether a legacy or start-up, should be asking itself - based on everything they've learned and know about AI and what Tery and Frank put forth - what does a meaningful response look like that aligns with our vision and values? What kind of world do we want to create? What's true to us and our continued success while motivating and useful to the people we serve?

For the past decade, many Fortune 500 brands have talked about and codified a "brand purpose" that aspired to make bigger and braver societal proclamations and contributions that better our lives, communities, and the world around us.

Now is the time to walk the talk and reflect on those ideals. Think strategically about how Ai can not only be used as a source for growth but equally one that fortifies trust between you and the people you serve.

This requires using AI as source for good – finding imaginative ways to keep doing what great brands have previously done – inspiring us to dream bigger while bettering our everyday experiences. And yes, the choice is ours or "yours" as to how you embrace and use AI.

Nelson Freitas, Founder, *Unknowns*

Fueling transformative brand potential, Nelson's decorated career spans three decades as a strategist working with iconic brands like Apple, Levi's, and Microsoft. His innovative leadership stretches across two of the world's most impactful communications and media companies, Omnicom and WPP, as Chief Strategy Officer.

Mentoring future trailblazers, Nelson brings his insights to Columbia University and NYU classrooms while also enlightening minds at industry meccas like Cannes and CES. His belief? Brands have the power to shape new realities, and distinct strengths can propel brands into uncharted frontiers of success.

Preface

Frank Sikernitsky, Founder, *Skyrocket Services*

With a fascination for AI now a household concept, I couldn't resist starting a consulting firm with some close colleagues named Skyrocket Services to help organizations navigate around this new and fraught space.

AI technology is advancing so quickly that it's hard to keep up. A single book would be out of date quickly, even if we only stuck to a particular subject or market.

With that in mind, we intend to update this book with a new edition each year. We will also keep a change log, to help document trends over time. AI capabilities, innovation and even government regulation will all combine to change the trajectory.

AI will undoubtedly impact our personal lives but more so businesses, which will need to change the way they operate to accommodate a radically different model of productivity. It's easy to pay $20 per month for ChatGPT and say, 'We have AI,' but the real value is having a comprehensive strategy down the road to transforming your business -- because your competitors are doing the same thing. They are exploring the existential risks to their business – issues like AI Collapse, Mutually Assured AI, and Alignment – and how to comprehensively manage them while moving forward. We'll get to all those very soon.

Inside The Ultimate Box

AI is a civilization-changing tool -- but not in all the ways the hype is painting it. It's true that AI will relegate most basic data processing and knowledge work to machines since its mostly just pattern matching and rule-filtering. This kind of automation of knowledge jobs was already happening long before generative AI burst onto the scene.

But the hype is far beyond that, frothed into ridiculous and frightening places. The hype says the danger isn't only to knowledge workers but writers, artists, parents, politicians, and CFOs, and just about anyone who isn't working in a trade.

Part of this is because the AI looks so capable. You talk to it, and it writes back with impeccable spelling and grammar and sounds knowledgeable.

But part of it is just the fear that well-funded PR machines use to punch up headlines. Not only has generative AI been developing for years, but it is also the next grudge match in the Microsoft vs. Google rivalry. Make no mistake, Redmond is well aware they were either late or utterly failed to convert on almost every 'next big thing' for 20 years; they lost browser, search, and mobile to Google.

It's not surprising that the media push was so huge that it pushed ChatGPT over the hump of hardcore tech media and into the mind of the ordinary public. "Here's something you can talk to, and if you're not an expert, it will seem to be an expert to you." As if that headline weren't enough, then the headlines claim 'and it will take your job' -- and you are guaranteed a click.

What is the reality here? As impressive as some of the output is, it is becoming clearer that LLMs are not great at things requiring imagination, creativity, empathy, or anything colloquially referred to as 'thinking outside the box.' It is impossible for an LLM to do those things. Why? Because LLMs were intentionally designed to be the ultimate box.

At their core, generative AIs do one very simple thing: complete a pattern. My apologies to the thousands of researchers and scientists out there for the simplification, I realize it's vastly more complicated...but then again, maybe not? The models are fed billions of parameters to be able to complete the largest variety of patterns in as many contexts as possible. So, their directives are deterministic: they must complete that pattern. In fact, it is so bent on completing a pattern that it may create one where there are none -- in other words, hallucinate.

But the machine won't intentionally go off its pattern. This means it cannot take a sidebar, develop a parallel thought, or weave in subtlety or nuance that it hasn't frequently seen before. It cannot make a leap between concepts not connected in its training.

So, the very thing that makes it savagely efficient at following a process that calls on lots of context and structure policy and data (e.g., most business processes), makes it lousy at being original (most creative work, a wide swath of 'good' management, product development, etc.)

The best it can do is get instructions to make a pattern that it hasn't seen, but the results are usually deeply underwhelming. Try asking it for an original Dad Joke. They manage to be even more lame than the real thing.

Mutually Assured AI

These days, it's easy to hot-drop some ChatGPT functions into a product, let the user generate prompts inside your app, and call the whole thing 'AI.' It's become a popular move among the droves of software-as-a-service providers who are trying to avoid down financing rounds in a tightening market. But it leads to what I call 'mutually assured AI' -- everyone has it. So, it's no longer a differentiator.

The use case is so trivial and unconnected to the core business that it no longer justifies its value. Every productivity package I use today has an AI menu option somewhere – many are in beta, and all new in the last 3 months. None of them help me better than using ChatGPT or Bard directly, except it's one less click. And some have the temerity to upsell me for it.

Where are the use cases that soak deeply into the business and transform it from the bottom up? Admittedly, we're in very early days here in 2023. Only a few novel use cases have started to crop up that are deeply tied to business architecture rather than floated on the surface.

Great Power and Greater Responsibility

AI comes with a rather large variety of dangers. Most are well-known; while some are hard to solve, others are entirely overblown.

The first is that this particular AI, or maybe next year's version, will kill us all. Returning to my sci-fi upbringing, we have been socialized to believe that advanced AI will invariably 'decide' to exterminate us. Skynet burns the Earth on Judgement Day. HAL-9000 murders its crew. The story that crystallizes this trope is the "Ultimate Computer" episode of the original Star Trek, wherein a big blinky talking computer is installed on the ship to make it fully automatic.

All crew but the senior officers are removed, ostensibly so they can grouse about their jobs being taken by a machine. But by the bottom half of the hour, the computer has committed the ship to a homicidal rampage because, of course, it would.

But what real-world risks does generative AI pose today, in 2023?

Generative AI models can generate realistic and convincing text, audio, video, and other media. This capability can be misused to create "deep fakes" (manipulated videos or images that appear real) or to spread false information or propaganda, leading to potential harm in areas like politics, business, and individual privacy. The same approach can be used to bolster fraud and break down security by making social engineering -- also known as 'fooling people' -- much faster and hard to spot.

These systems have the potential to generate content that may be offensive, defamatory, or harmful. Even when this is unintentional, it can lead to ethical issues. Similarly, using AI to create artwork, music, or writing raises questions about authorship and intellectual property.

AI models, like GPT-4, are trained on massive amounts of data, some of which can be sensitive, private, biased or just plain wrong. Although trainers claim efforts are made to avoid using identifiable information, there's a risk that some information could be included or inferred.

Most of all, Generative AI models could generate unpredictable and unexpected results, given their complexity and the nuances of the tasks they are assigned. These models may inadvertently produce harmful or inappropriate content, make bad recommendations, omit crucial information, or otherwise act in ways that cause unintended negative outcomes.

Each of these leads directly to traditional business risks: execution risk, financial risk, and reputational risk. The challenge is for organizations to choose models trained in alignment with their goals and integrated into systems that control the risks they pose. Again, dropping a pop-up AI autocomplete box onto the corporate intranet doesn't begin to scratch the surface of what a serious AI deployment looks like.

AI Collapse

Developing AI apps and systems also has one particular risk that's new and very unique to generative AI. It's called collapse, and it goes something like this:

In the past, tech often innovated in the niches that big platforms provided. People built new functions on top of Windows, or iOS or SalesForce. These niche opportunities only existed for a few years, but they had big value -- until the platform offered them natively, and the opportunity was suddenly gone.

But LLMs and generative AI are moving so quickly that the better mousetrap is often just days away. "Collapse" refers to generative models (and the tech around them) adding so much capability in 'the next version' that they consume all the custom work developers constructed on top of earlier models. A timeline:

Week 0

Somebody builds a tool that does something novel, like ingesting a variety of proprietary marketing PDFs, tying in a design workflow with a visualization package, and letting the AI auto-design company PowerPoint templates. It's an awesome demo. Everyone loves it.

Week 2

That exact feature set appears in a repo on GitHub, and it gets 1,000 stars daily. Hundreds clone it and run it.

Week 5

Three almost identical startups begin offering that exact feature set under slick but generally identical interfaces. Of course, they offer it as-a-service for $10/mo.

Week 9

OpenAI and/or Google (or AWS or whoever) announce that the latest model improvements will handle that exact workflow and export to PPT, in a single prompt, for no added cost, inside the tools everyone already uses. Two weeks later, open-source models catch up, so it's free if you want to host it.

In less than a fiscal quarter, we've seen the entire cycle. Exploiting niches for-profit used to take years. Now those bubbles of opportunity last weeks. Even Microsoft and Apple would take years to consume useful features that smaller developers deployed. Betting on individual AI features isn't classic technical debt – it's actually technical roulette.

The Lesson

Chasing features may be a fine pursuit for engineers, but bigger organizations need to build strategies that account for collapse, security, accountability, ethics, business sustainability, and transparency.

Measuring Up

This book is about understanding generative AI for what it really is and leveraging that capability to catapult brands and businesses ahead.

However, one must be careful how that's done. The very first step is to truly understand how your own business is structured, measured, and rewarded. Keeping in mind the way most corporations are traditionally incentivized today, here's a hypothetical, if simplified, story (that's based on an interview question I've been asking candidates for 15 years):

Imagine you have Company A1. There's a team of 100 people, each paid $100K, each making the company $200K. So, $20M revenue -$10M cost = $10M profit.

AI comes along and enables every 1 person to do the job of 5. So Manager X buys the software, say it costs $1M, and lays off 4 out of every 5 people. Now it's:

> 20 people, each paid $100K, making the company $1M each (5x200) means that the group is making the same $20M revenue minus $2M for salary and the $1M for the software – resulting in a $17M profit. It's a 70% increase in profit.

Manager X, and his Manager, Y, party it up because the way they're incentivized, they get paid for collecting skulls and cutting costs. There are promotions and bonuses, and all is happiness and mirth. The legendary tale is told through huge slide decks at the corporate retreat. They're so much "leaner and meaner" while facing a huge and growing market. But the reality is that X just made a fatal error, and Y's endorsement will doom the company to failure.

Imagine their competitor did something different. Company B2 spent $1M on AI but kept all 100 people. So, they still have a $10M payroll plus the $1M software, but they're able to support 100M in revenue, so $79M will be profit. That's a 790% increase in profit.

The discrepancy is staggering -- in this theoretical 'huge and growing market,' in less than a year, we can imagine company B2 buying company A1 and firing Managers X and Y and their boss, Z, too. It's a complete flameout.

The headline is that AI is best used as a multiplier, not a divisor. People hanging onto discredited business dogma from the 80s and 90s about 'synergistic efficiencies' and 'rightsizing headcount' will be ground to dust by the new reality, which is the expansion of the capacity, capability, and of speed -- of human work output. AI is just a force multiplier. It will also require new metrics and methods for judging success lest a team thinks they're succeeding when they're actually jumping off a cliff.

Good, Fast, or Cheap?

There's a wide space between dropping in AI and transforming using AI. It's quite simple to do the former -- any one of a thousand startups will take your enterprise license fee and give you a plug-in. But transforming your organization to benefit from AI, bottom-up, is a bigger job -- with a much heftier payout.

The examples of Companies A1 and B2 may be simplistic, but they are roughly the paths organizations have to choose from. One can build the perfect lean and efficient company in the definition of the 20th century -- in other words, be the shiniest, best-looking, best audited dinosaur fossils around.

Or one can use AI, rightly understood, to double down in the 21st century and expand everyone's capabilities. These organizations will choose this path because it's how business will work in the coming decades, but also because that's what their competitors -- your competitors -- are doing now.

Bring the Skyrocket

This exciting time is why we started Skyrocket. It feels like the early Web days when there were shallow moats, and the future was for imagining. We realize it's more fraught -- this time around, there's more risk, and more seems to be at stake. AI leverage in business automation is so extreme that it's clearly more critical to 'get this right' than ever before.

But as in the early Web days, we can build on bedrock. We can have control of the direction this goes in. We at Skyrocket have decades of experience building and creating, and working for many of the biggest and best that came out of that last huge paradigm shift. We understand the technology and its effects on the nature of work and productivity.

We at Skyrocket are looking to solve these deeper questions. We want to help organizations create the roadmap, policy, and solutions to change whole industries, not merely do sideshow tricks on a right click. And we want to help as many organizations as we can reap these benefits, rightly understood.

Point of View on AI

In AI for Brands: Embracing the Future, three visionary authors unite, sharing exclusive insights on generative AI for businesses and brands. Each author delivers an exhilarating exploration into the unveiled potential of AI, guiding the reader through the cutting-edge terrain where AI becomes an instrumental driver of growth. Embrace change; seize command; unleash innovation – the mantra for success in the AI-powered era. Adapt. Dominate. Innovate.

Adapt, Dominate, and Innovate form the cornerstone of our vision for a future shaped by AI in branding and marketing:

Adapt: As we navigate the dawn of the AI era, flexibility is paramount. The constant flux in AI technology demands that businesses and brands remain agile and receptive to new strategies. Adaptability fostered by ongoing learning and responsiveness assures survival in this competitive landscape.

Dominate: Information is power in the AI-driven world. Harnessing advanced AI tools not only offers deep insights into customer behavior but also enables brands to tailor their approach, outmaneuver the competition, and effectively dominate their market niche.

Innovate: The transformative power of AI lies in its endless ability to innovate. It can unearth new models of interaction, new paths to customer engagement, and even new product realms. Embracing AI allows room for continuous innovation, setting a brand's trajectory above and beyond.

Tery Spataro

The ever-evolving landscape of Artificial Intelligence (AI) holds immense promise for revolutionizing numerous industries. As an ardent explorer of AI for over two decades, I am delighted to share my inspiring journey with you.

The convergence of creativity and branding offers a myriad of possibilities, ranging from leveraging algorithms to optimize processes, predictions, and customer relationships, to developing groundbreaking concepts that elevate brands with the aid of generative AI. Undoubtedly, AI is actively shaping the future of brands. Together, let us embark on this invigorating adventure and see the transformative impact of AI!

My exploration of AI began 23 years ago, during its nascent stages. The boundless potential of AI and its ability to reshape our world fascinated me. Throughout the years, I witnessed remarkable advancements, from the development of intricate algorithms to the creation of advanced machine-learning models. As an inquisitive individual driven by innovation, I am thrilled to share my journey and insights with you.

The digital age has ushered in unparalleled connectivity and access to information, redefining how we communicate, work, and live. It is this fascination with the digital realm, technology, and the internet that fueled my intrigue in AI and its applications across various domains, including branding.

Algorithms serve as the foundation of AI, empowering machines to learn, adapt, and evolve. By harnessing the power of algorithms, brands can unlock a multitude of opportunities to enhance their operations, make informed predictions, and cultivate deeper connections with their customers.

Efficiency plays a pivotal role in the realm of branding. Brands must continuously strive to optimize their processes, ensuring they remain competitive and deliver exceptional experiences to their customers. AI-powered algorithms can contribute significantly to this pursuit by streamlining operations and reducing costs.

For instance, brands can automate repetitive tasks using AI algorithms, freeing up valuable time and resources for more strategic initiatives. Additionally, AI can optimize supply chain management, ensuring the most efficient and cost-effective production and delivery of products.

Moreover, AI algorithms possess the capability to analyze extensive data sets, unveiling patterns and trends that inform decision-making. This analytical prowess can lead to more effective marketing campaigns, enhanced product development, and improved overall business performance. The ability to predict trends and consumer behavior is paramount in successful branding. Brands that accurately anticipate the needs and desires of their customers are positioned to develop compelling products and marketing campaigns that deeply resonate with their target audience.

AI algorithms substantially enhance a brand's predictive capabilities by analyzing vast amounts of data, identifying intricate patterns that may elude human analysts. The recognition of these patterns facilitates more accurate forecasts, enabling brands to make well-informed decisions concerning product development, marketing strategies, and other critical business initiatives.

Furthermore, AI-powered prediction tools aid brands in identifying potential risks and opportunities, enabling proactive measures to address challenges and capitalize on emerging trends. This adaptability ensures brands remain agile and responsive within the ever-changing business landscape.

Building robust and enduring customer relationships is essential for any brand striving for long-term success. In today's fiercely competitive marketplace, where consumers have an abundance of choices, brands must cultivate loyalty and trust among their customer base.

AI algorithms play a pivotal role in helping brands forge and support strong customer relationships. By analyzing customer data, AI provides valuable insights into individual preferences, behaviors, and needs, allowing brands to deliver highly personalized experiences that resonate deeply with their audience.

Additionally, AI-powered customer service tools, such as chatbots and virtual assistants, enable brands to provide timely and efficient support, addressing inquiries and resolving issues promptly. This heightened customer satisfaction and loyalty ultimately benefit the brand's bottom line.

Two decades after embarking on my AI journey, I embraced generative AI to augment my creative process. As I delved further into the realm of AI, I discovered the incredible potential of generative AI in fostering creativity and pushing the boundaries of branding. Generative AI uses algorithms to generate original content, such as images, text, music, and even entire concepts, without explicit human input. This technology has opened up new avenues for brands to create unique, compelling, and innovative content.

Generative AI algorithms can learn from vast datasets and generate content that imitates the style, tone, and aesthetics of a brand. For example, these algorithms can analyze a brand's existing visual assets, such as logos, images, and design elements, and generate new visuals that align seamlessly with the brand's identity.

This capability is particularly valuable when it comes to scaling creative efforts. With generative AI, brands can automate the production of content, such as social media graphics or website banners, while keeping consistency and adhering to the brand guidelines. This not only saves time and resources but also ensures a cohesive and professional brand presence across different platforms.

Moreover, generative AI can spark creativity and inspire new ideas. By exposing AI algorithms to diverse datasets and providing them with creative constraints, brands can generate a wide range of novel concepts and explore uncharted territories. These generated concepts can serve as a starting point for human creatives, who can then refine and develop them further, resulting in unique and innovative branding initiatives.

One area where generative AI has gained significant attention is in the field of content creation. AI-powered tools can generate written content, such as product descriptions, white paper, blog and social media posts, based on a given topic or set of keywords. While human input is still valuable for crafting the final output, generative AI can provide a starting point or generate multiple variations to choose from, saving time and effort in the content creation process.

However, it's important to note that while generative AI offers exciting possibilities, it is crucial to keep a balance between algorithm and human creativity. AI algorithms are powerful tools, but they should be seen as collaborators rather than replacements for human creatives. The human touch, intuition, and subjective judgment are still invaluable when it comes to crafting compelling brand stories and connecting with audiences on an emotional level.

Generative AI holds immense potential for transforming the branding landscape. By leveraging algorithms to optimize processes, enhance predictions, and foster creativity, brands can gain a competitive edge and establish deeper connections with their customers. As we continue to explore the vastness of AI, I am excited to witness the ongoing evolution and its profound impact on the world of branding.

As we stand on the precipice of a new era for brands, we must come together to embrace the AI revolution. By fostering collaboration, education, and responsible AI development, we can exploit AI's power to revolutionize how we approach branding and create a brighter, more equitable future for all.

I invite you to join me on this exciting journey as we explore the possibilities of AI and unlock its full potential for our brands and society. Let's embrace the AI revolution and create a world where technology, creativity, and human connection coalesce to drive innovation, growth, and positive change.

Frank Sikernitsky

Since I was a child, I have had a fascination with Artificial Intelligence. Maybe it was all the sci-fi I was brought up on or seeing computers turning up in homes as personal devices.

But it stayed with me. Even though I was pursuing a political science degree at college, I took neuroscience and artificial intelligence courses. Even 30 years ago, it was a fascinating subject. I built voice skills for Amazon and Google to try out NLP. And just in the last 6 months, I've watched generative AI break through the years of steady progress into the public consciousness.

Tool-building is what differentiates us from other animals (although we now know this is not strictly true, it's a matter of scale: we do not see dolphins buying socket drivers at Ace Hardware.)

So, we build ever more powerful tools. The wheel, the cotton gin, the petrochemical refinery, the hydrogen bomb, Disco, the digital watch, the supercomputer, the Internet, etc.

Large learning models are tools too and I'm little surprised that this kind of AI surprised so many people. I'm talking specifically about generative AI since we've had branches of

AI developing at different rates for decades. For example, fuzzy logic has been a legitimate branch of AI technology that's been actively developed for 25 years. It forms the basis of many of the control systems in our cars (namely the automatic transmissions and other "learning" systems) in even the lowliest of applications.

But it's no longer referred to as a big deal in AI. I think the "AI" moniker comes with whatever is exciting at the moment, and we've reached another one...so back to this "eureka moment"...

We can rewrite DNA, populate Mars with nothing but robots, eradicate two dozen diseases and manage dozens more that were all fatal 100 years ago and some as recently as 20 years ago. We can split atoms, prevent food from spoiling for years, and

We beam signals into space in the altruistic but somehow slightly sad hope to hear back that we're not alone.

So why be surprised by technology now? I believe it's because we didn't care before. Machines were things of sci-fi and you always had to suspend belief a little to buy the plot.

But the hype and the shock (manufactured or not) keep this crop of generative AI at the forefront of public discourse. And it's unique that this branch of AI has passed into the general public's view.

Beyond the hype, I think it's the idea that something not altogether human is talking back to us in clear cogent English – which most of our colleagues and coworkers don't always manage.

Generative AI touches something instinctive in humans. It's a visceral reaction when something that's not human interacts with you. We've all heard of the Turing test but it always seemed so dry (and subjective) – until you're playing with a chat screen that's coming close. At the beginning I found myself steeped in the childlike sense of wonder which is the best litmus test for new technology.

Does it make you feel like a kid in the sheer joy of a new thing to play with? Then that turns into "stupid tricks" phase – this is typified by the hundreds of similar posts on social media explaining today's 1000 new prompts or how to ask subtly different questions or get it to say bad things or act strangely. But even that passes into:

"What is this really? And understanding it for what it really is, what can we use this for?"

The kicker is the technology itself can be asked what we can use it for. And the irony is that it will tell us what the breadth and width of the internet has already decided it's good for. So, as far as its training is concerned, we're in the early days. GPT-4 is out and the old saying in the boxed software world was that no application was even worth looking at until version 4 or 5.

I'm attracted to AI because we're in the early days. We're playing with a technology that builds on bedrock so to speak, it's like early web days in many ways:

The use cases are just emerging.

Resources are scarce and expensive so efficiency will be key.

There's no one gatekeeper.

There is more than one value proposition.

Mobile and social arrived in the interim but they worked within walled gardens. Somebody had control from a root level so there wasn't bedrock underneath, there was an opaque framework. These days black box AI exists but so do open-source ones you can run on your own machinery.

So, in terms of value propositions, AI has room to move in unexpected directions. This is really why it's interesting to me. Communities and individual creativity really count here, and nobody has cornered the market in experience or knowledge.

It will be a be a fun ten years while everyone figures this out. Anyone who tells you they have the technical solution right now probably doesn't – follow instead the people (like Skyrocket) looking to expand the value by applying it in new ways, to new problems.

Whitney Tindale

AI has been around for some time now and what started in the imaginations of science fiction writers has morphed into reality on many fronts.

I've spent the lion's share of my career running the operations of investment advisory businesses and I have seen firsthand the benefits and efficiency gains that are possible for businesses that embrace and adopt technology, including AI, in its infancy.

Much of the early machine learning AI software was limited to clever logic-based algorithms – essentially highly functional if/then coding. Despite its relative simplicity, this basic software turned out to be extremely useful and productivity software was rapidly adopted in the middle and back offices of most midsize and large businesses.

This widespread adoption simplified or replaced many of the manual processes that were expensive, time-consuming and subject to human error. The software was so successful that people began to wonder "What happened to Phil in accounting?" At some of the larger companies, Phil was most likely replaced by the robotic process automation software he trained. At others, Phil was probably so overworked that the help he got from AI would allow him to take a vacation.

The next phase of AI adoption continues today with the much more sophisticated Large Language Models that have led to Generative AI (e.g., Chat GPT, DALL-E, and their ilk). These modern products focus on communication AI and are so good at writing prose and generating images that their output is generally indistinguishable from high-quality human output.

While the first wave of AI came for the middle and back-office processes, Generative AI is coming for everything else, including the marketing and branding departments. Despite the negative headlines about job losses, I think it will be good for society.

Why do I say that? Because we are currently participating in the 4th industrial revolution and throttling progress has never been a win for mankind (think of the benefits we've obtained from generating and harnessing electricity, creating industrial processes like assembly lines, or discovering and inventing things like antibiotics, telecommunications, computers, etc.). While we may need some guardrails on AI at some point, talk of it triggering the end of the world seems overdone (personally, I think the military's wetware is a bigger threat to the world than AI's software, but we'll save that discussion for another time).

So where do we go from here? There will surely be massive productivity gains associated with the use of Generative AI and the new ways companies will perform corporate tasks. In 2018, the technology guru, Benedict Scott, described using Machine Learning software as having access to an infinite number of 10-year-old interns. That was long before the public availability of the much more powerful Generative AI.

Fast forward to today and the 10-year-old interns are all grown up. They communicate like scholars and draw like da Vinci (or any other master). Best of all, they come armed with most of the "knowledge" humans saw fit to write down. They also do everything at the speed of "done". Their only weakness is they are a little precocious and tend to hallucinate. They can also provide inaccurate answers if they aren't fed enough data or if "the right answer" isn't obvious or changes frequently. That can happen in industries that evolve quickly (e.g., technology) or operate in environments with frequently changing rules (e.g., legal, tax, or highly regulated businesses). In short, like all interns, AI needs some adult supervision from an experienced mentor.

Similar to what we saw in the first three industrial revolutions, I expect society will experience net gains from AI that will make the changes worth it – even though there will be winners and losers.

At the company level, the question will be how to create and spend the productivity gains. Will companies use Generative AI to reduce headcount and shift income from the employees to the shareholders, or will the productivity gains be used for corporate growth and/or to provide customers with a better product or experience? The answers will vary by company and probably by industry.

At this point, it seems kind of obvious that companies will have to incorporate Generative AI in their operations just to keep up with their competitors. The question is when and how best to implement this wonderful new technology. I think it's okay to start slowly with single-purpose software and work towards custom solutions if the budget and available expertise allow for it. I suspect the sooner companies get started the less catching up they'll have to do.

Lastly, I would be betraying my career in operations and compliance if I didn't provide a couple of quick caveats. Like all important technology projects, things can go sideways quickly if all the stakeholders in the project aren't brought in early (legal, compliance, tech, regulators, etc.). It's better to get early buy-in from the whole team as Generative AI comes with a host of potential problems (e.g., things like copyright ownership of the data used in the models, inadvertently sharing private or personally identifiable information on public models, etc.).

All that said, it's time to move forward. Game on!

Any sufficiently advanced technology is indistinguishable from magic.

- Arthur C. Clarke

Introduction

The rise of artificial intelligence (AI)

In recent years, artificial intelligence has become integral part of our everyday lives, whether we realize it or not. From personal assistants like Bard and Alexa to self-driving vehicles, AI is changing the way we live, work, and interact with technology. This rapid growth of AI has also had a profound impact on the world of branding and marketing, opening new opportunities and challenges for businesses looking to adapt to this ever-evolving landscape.

The rise of artificial intelligence has undoubtedly transformed various aspects of our lives, bringing convenience, efficiency, and a wealth of new possibilities. As AI continues to develop, brands and marketers need to stay ahead of the curve, by embracing the changes and using AI to its fullest potential.

The impact of AI on brands and marketing

Staying up to date with AI developments is essential for businesses striving to maintain a competitive edge. By staying knowledgeable and adaptable, companies can exploit AI's potential to foster creativity, improve customer relations, and promote long-term prosperity.

The emergence of artificial intelligence is undoubtedly revolutionizing the branding and marketing industry, presenting both novel prospects and obstacles. By comprehending the intricacies of AI and integrating it into their methods, brands can not only keep pace with the competition but also exploit this groundbreaking technology to augment their overall customer engagement and industry standing. With AI evolving continuously, its applications in branding and marketing appear boundless, ushering in a new epoch of ingenuity and expansion for organizations worldwide.

The importance of understanding AI for brands

AI is changing the future of branding and marketing, it is essential to understand the potential benefits and challenges associated with AI technology. By staying informed and adaptable, brands can successfully navigate this new frontier and embrace AI as a valuable tool for growth and innovation.

Understanding and adapting to the advancements in AI technology is crucial for brands that wish to remain competitive in the market. By staying informed and agile, businesses can leverage the power of AI to drive innovation, increase customer satisfaction, and achieve sustainable growth.

The rise of artificial intelligence is undeniably reshaping the world of branding and marketing, offering new opportunities as well as challenges. By understanding the implications of AI and incorporating it into the strategies, brands can not only stay ahead in the game but also capitalize on this technological revolution to enhance their overall customer experience and market positioning. As AI continues to develop and mature, the possibilities for its application in branding and marketing are virtually limitless, opening up a new era of innovation and growth for businesses across the globe.

Embracing the Future: AI for Brands is a strategic guide for helping brands understand what it will take to become AI ready and taking the mystery out of using AI.

IT'S THE
REAL THING

I. What Brands Need to Know About Using AI

Essential AI Terms for Brands Venturing into the World of Artificial Intelligence

As artificial intelligence (AI) continues to revolutionize industries across the globe, it has become increasingly important for brands to familiarize themselves with its associated terminology and the key AI terms before integrating AI into their business strategies. By mastering these terms, brands will be better prepared to navigate the complex landscape of artificial intelligence to understand its full potential.

Artificial Intelligence (AI)

AI refers to the development of computer systems that can mimic and perform tasks that typically require human intelligence, such as visual perception, speech recognition, decision-making, and language translation. There are two primary types of AI: Narrow AI, which is designed for a specific task, and General AI, which has the capability to perform any cognitive task a human can do.

Machine Learning (ML)

Machine learning involves training computer algorithms to improve their performance on a task through experience. This is achieved by feeding the algorithm large amounts of data, allowing it to identify patterns and make predictions based on those patterns.

Deep Learning

A more advanced form of machine learning is Deep Learning, which uses artificial neural networks to model complex patterns in data. These networks are designed to mimic the structure and function of the human brain and are particularly effective at processing large amounts of unstructured data. These unstructured items such as text, images, audio, and video.

Natural Language Processing (NLP)

Natural Language Processing (NLP) is a division of AI with focus on the interaction between computers and human languages. It enables machines to understand, interpret, and generate human language in ways that are meaningful and useful. NLP is commonly used in applications such as chatbots, sentiment analysis, and language translation.

Computer Vision

Computer vision is another subfield of AI that deals with the processing and understanding of digital images and videos. It enables machines to identify and interpret visual information from the world, such as recognizing objects, faces, and scenes. Computer vision has many applications, including image recognition, video surveillance, and self-driving cars.

Neural Networks

Neural networks are a type of machine learning model inspired by the human brain's configuration and function. They consist of interconnected layers of artificial neurons, which process and transmit information. Neural networks are particularly effective at identifying patterns in large, complex data sets and are commonly used in deep learning applications.

Data Mining

Data mining is the process of detecting patterns and relationships in large data sets using machine learning, statistical analysis, and database systems. It helps businesses to identify valuable insights and make informed decisions based on the data they collect.

Algorithm

An algorithm is a set of rules or instructions that a computer follows to perform a specific task. In the context of AI, algorithms are used to process data, detect patterns, and make predictions or decisions based on those patterns.

Supervised Learning

Supervised learning is a type of machine learning in which an algorithm is trained on a labeled data set, meaning each data point includes both the input and the desired output. The algorithm learns to make predictions by comparing its output to the correct output and adjusting its parameters accordingly.

Unsupervised Learning

Unsupervised learning, on the other hand, consist of training an algorithm on an unlabeled data set. The algorithm must identify patterns and relationships within the data on its own, without any guidance regarding the desired output. This type of learning is particularly useful for discovering hidden structures and patterns within complex data sets.

Understanding these essential AI terms is crucial for brands seeking to incorporate artificial intelligence into their business strategies. By becoming familiar with these concepts, brands will be better equipped to make educated decisions regarding AI implementation and leverage its capabilities to drive innovation and growth in their respective industries.

Generative Adversarial Network (GAN)

A Generative Adversarial (GAN) is a class of machine learning systems that consists of two neural networks: a generator and a discriminator, that engage in a sort of competition. The generator creates new data samples, and the discriminator evaluates the authenticity of those samples. The goal of the generator is to produce data that is indistinguishable from real data, while the discriminator tries to correctly identify if the data is real or generated. This process continues iteratively, with the generator and discriminator improving their capabilities, leading to the generation of high-quality synthetic data.

Creative Adversarial Network (CAN)

A Creative Adversarial (CAN) is a type of GAN designed specifically for creating original and aesthetically pleasing artwork. The key difference between a traditional GAN and a CAN is the discriminator's role. In a CAN, the discriminator not only evaluates the authenticity of the generated artwork but also assesses its novelty and artistic quality. This encourages the generator to produce unique and aesthetically appealing pieces of art, rather than simply replicating existing artwork.

Generative Pre-trained Transformer (GPT)

Generative Pre-trained Transformer GPT is a type of deep learning model that utilizes a transformer architecture, which is designed to handle sequential data more effectively than other models, such as recurrent neural networks (RNNs). GPT is pre-trained on substantial amounts of text data and can be fine-tuned for numerous natural language processing jobs, such as machine translation, summarization, and question-answering. GPT has proven to be highly effective at generating coherent and contextually relevant text, making it a powerful tool for applications in text-based AI systems.

Algorithm

An algorithm is a step-by-step procedure or set of instructions for solving a problem or accomplishing a specific task. In computer science, algorithms are used to process data, perform calculations, and make decisions. They form the basis for all computer programs and are essential in fields such as artificial intelligence, machine learning, and data science. Algorithms can vary in complexity and are often evaluated based on their efficiency, accuracy, and speed.

Understanding the Types of Generated Outputs

As artificial intelligence continues to advance, brands are finding new and innovative ways to incorporate AI into their marketing strategies, product designs, and customer experiences. This fusion of technology and creativity has led to the emergence of various types of AI art that can add a unique and captivating touch to a brand's offerings. Here, we will discuss some of the different types of AI-generated art that brands can create.

Generative Adversarial Networks (GANs) Art

GANs are a type of AI algorithm that can generate realistic and visually stunning images by pitting two neural networks against each other. One network, the generator, creates the images, while the other, the discriminator, evaluates their quality. Brands can use GANs to create unique and engaging visual content for advertising campaigns, social media posts, or product packaging.

Style Transfer Art

Style transfer is an AI technique that allows brands to combine the content of one image with the style of another, resulting in a unique and visually striking piece of art. This technique enables brands to create personalized and on-brand visual content by applying their signature style to a variety of images, such as photographs, illustrations, or logos.

AI-Generated Music and Soundscapes

AI can also be used to generate original music and soundscapes, offering brands a unique way to enhance their audio branding or create immersive customer experiences. By training AI algorithms on various music genres, styles, and patterns, brands can generate custom soundtracks or jingles that resonate with their target audience.

Text-Based Art

Natural Language Processing (NLP) algorithms can generate text-based art, such as poetry, stories, or even interactive narratives. Brands can employ these AI-generated texts to create engaging and personalized content for marketing campaigns, product descriptions, or social media posts.

Fractal Art

Fractal art is generated using mathematical

algorithms that produce intricate and visually captivating patterns. These patterns can be customized and adapted to fit a brand's aesthetic, making them an excellent choice for creating distinctive visual elements for marketing materials, product designs, or website backgrounds.

AI-Assisted Design

AI can be used to enhance creative practices by offering design suggestions or automating repetitive tasks, allowing designers to focus on more critical aspects of their work.

Brands can leverage AI-assisted design tools to create more effective and visually appealing designs for their marketing materials, products, or digital platforms.

Data Visualization

Agorithms can be used to analyze and visualize complex data sets, transforming raw data into visually engaging and easy-to-understand graphics. Brands can use these AI-generated data visualizations to communicate important information or insights to their customers, stakeholders, or employees in a visually compelling manner.

Copy

There are many AI tools available for generating copy, each with their own capabilities and features. These tools leverage advanced algorithms and techniques to create content for different purposes, such as marketing copy, slogans, product descriptions, social media captions, and more. Some AI tools use prompts to generate text within existing applications, while others are designed to learn from data and generate original content. As generative AI continues to evolve, can expect to see even more sophisticated solutions for producing high-quality content without specifically endorsing any individual tool. The possibilities for AI-generated art and copy are vast and continuously expanding. By experimenting with different types of AI art, brands can create captivating and unique visual content setting them apart from their competitors and engages their target audience.

AI is in a evolutionary mode, as it improves, we can expect to see even more innovative and creative applications in the world of art and design.

The Different Types of AI Technologies

There is more to AI than just clicking a button. There are several key types of AI technologies that can be used by brands to enhance their strategies and operations.

Keep in mind, AI is a broad category of technologies that can be used to make machines think, act, and interact like humans. There are many different types of AI technologies, but all work together to achieve the same goal--to create machines that can think for themselves.

AI has been around since the 1950s when computer scientists first started working on creating computers capable of understanding language and making decisions based on their surroundings (like humans do).

Machine Learning (ML)

Machine learning (ML) is a type of algorithm that

allows systems to learn from data and make predictions. It's often used in conjunction with other technologies, like deep learning and neural networks, but it can also be used on its own.

Machine learning involves training a system to perform tasks by feeding it large amounts of information and providing feedback on whether or not its output was correct. For example: if you want your computer to recognize faces in photos, you'd give it thousands upon thousands of pictures with people's faces in them--and tell the computer whether each one had someone's face or not (i.e., "this one has a face"). Then over time the computer will start making its own decisions based on what information it already knows about faces (for example: they're usually round).

Deep Learning

Deep learning, a subset of machine learning, uses neural networks to learn patterns from data. A neural network consists of layers, each with nodes and connections between them. When you feed information into the first layer, it passes it along to the next layer, which processes it in turn and feeds its output to subsequent layers until you reach the end of your data set (or "output").

The advantage of deep learning over other types of AI technologies is that it can learn from large amounts of data without needing human intervention or supervision--you just give your computer enough examples from which to draw conclusions about how different things are related, then let it do its thing!

Natural Language Processing (NLP)

Natural language processing (NLP) is the capability of a computer to understand human language. It's an AI technology that can be used in various applications such as chatbots, search engines, and voice assistants like Siri and Alexa. Natural language processing utilizes several techniques including:

Natural Language Understanding (NLU) - This involves understanding the intent behind a user's input. For example, when you say "I want to go home," your phone understands that you want to navigate back home on Google Maps or Apple Maps; however if you said "I want my mommy," it would not know what action should take place next because there are many ways this could be interpreted by humans. Depending on context such as whether someone else was around at the time of speaking those words aloud versus typing them into their phone screen. Using voice commands alone without having any other people present nearby at all times during conversation time periods between two separate individuals who may or may not have been communicating with each other face-to-face before making contact via text messaging platforms such as Facebook Messenger app which allows users access services such as sending messages between friends without needing internet connections available at all times since most phones nowadays come equipped with built-in Wi-Fi capabilities so long as they're connected properly through cables plugged directly into outlets located throughout homes all across America today."

Computer Vision

Computer vision is a branch of artificial intelligence that deals with the creation and use of algorithms to allow computers to gain high-level understanding from digital images or videos. Computer vision can be used in many applications including image recognition, object tracking, facial recognition, video analysis and more.

Neural Networks

Neural networks are a type of artificial intelligence that mimics the brain's neural structure.

Neural networks are used for image recognition, speech recognition and many other tasks where you want to teach computers how to learn from data.

The idea behind neural networks is that they can be trained with examples (e.g., pictures) so that they can make predictions about new data.

Large Language Models

A large language model (LLM) is a type of artificial intelligence algorithm that uses deep learning techniques and massively large data sets to understand, summarize, generate and predict new content. LLMs are designed to recognize, summarize, translate, predict, create text, and other types of content based on knowledge gained from enormous amounts of datasets. Essentially, LLMs are designed to be able to understand natural language and produce human-like responses.

Large language models are important to brands, for several reasons. Firstly, LLMs can be used to automate many processes, such as sentiment analysis, customer service, content creation, fraud detection, prediction and classification, which leads to reduced manual labor and related costs. Secondly, LLMs can help brands to personalize their interactions with customers by processing large amounts of data to create targeted and relevant content. Using LLM content could lead to increased customer engagement and loyalty. Lastly, LLMs can be used in marketing research to analyze large amounts of customer data, which can help brands to better understand their customers and improve their products and services.

How AI can enhance brand strategy

In the digital landscape is constantly changing, AI technologies have emerged as a game-changer for brands seeking to enhance their strategies and foster deeper connections with their customers. By utilizing the potential of AI, businesses can unlock a multitude of benefits, including personalized marketing efforts, streamlined content creation, and data-driven decision-making. These cutting-edge tools empower brands to deliver exceptional customer experiences, optimize their online presence, and stay ahead of the competition, ultimately driving long-term success and growth. As we delve deeper into the applications of AI in brand strategy, we will explore the key advantages of personalization and customer segmentation, content creation and curation, and predictive analytics, demonstrating the transformative potential of these technologies in shaping the future of branding and marketing.

AI technologies offer several benefits to brands looking to improve their strategies and connect with customers on a deeper level.

Personalization and customer segmentation: One of the most significant advantages of using AI in brand strategy is the ability to personalize marketing efforts and segment customers based on their behavior, preferences, and needs. By analyzing vast amounts of customer data through machine learning algorithms, AI can identify patterns in customer behavior, enabling brands to create more personalized content, products, and services. This level of personalization leads to increased customer engagement and loyalty, as customers feel better understood and valued. Additionally, customer segmentation allows brands to tailor their marketing and communication efforts to specific customer groups, ensuring that the right message reaches the target audience, ultimately leading to better conversion rates and higher customer satisfaction.

Content creation and curation: AI-powered content creation tools, use NLP and M algorithms, can help brands develop engaging and relevant content for their audiences. These tools are used to generate ideas, optimize headlines, and even write articles or social media posts in a fraction of the time it would take a human writer. AI can also assist with content curation by filtering through the vast amount of information available on the internet and selecting the most relevant and valuable pieces for a brand's target audience. This process can streamlined the content strategy that caters to the interests of the audience and showcases the brand's expertise in their industry.

Predictive analytics and data-driven decision making: Machine learning and deep learning algorithms can analyze historical data and predict future trends, customer behavior, and market dynamics. This enables brands to make more informed, data-driven decisions in their marketing and business strategies. By leveraging AI-powered predictive analytics, businesses can identify potential opportunities, risks, and areas for improvement, allowing businesses be nimble and stay ahead of the competition. This proactive approach to decision-making ensures that brands remain relevant and agile in an ever-evolving market landscape, improving their overall brand positioning and long-term success.

Integrating AI in marketing and advertising

The integration of AI in marketing and advertising has unleashed a new era of efficiency, precision, and innovation, enabling businesses to connect with their target audiences like never before. By making use of the power of AI, brands can revolutionize their marketing strategies, delivering highly personalized experiences and ensuring optimal resource allocation. In this section, we will explore the various ways AI can be seamlessly integrated into marketing and advertising efforts, including programmatic advertising, chatbots and virtual assistants, and social media sentiment analysis, highlighting the transformative impact of these technologies on today's marketing landscape.

Programmatic advertising: AI-driven programmatic advertising has changed the game for digital ad buying and placement. Machine learning algorithms can analyze vast amounts of data, and optimize ad purchases, placements, and bids in real-time. This ensures that brands reach the right audiences at the right time with the most relevant content. Programmatic advertising offers numerous benefits, such as increased efficiency, reduced costs, and better targeting, ultimately leading to higher return on investment (ROI) for advertising campaigns.

Chatbots and virtual assistants: One of the most visible applications of AI in marketing and advertising is the use of chatbots and virtual assistants. Chatbots and virtual assistants can engage with customers, provide personalized support, answer frequently asked questions, and even make product recommendations based on individual preferences. By automating customer interactions, chatbots can streamline the customer service process, reducing response times, increasing customer satisfaction, and freeing up valuable resources for other tasks. Moreover, the continuous learning capabilities of AI enable chatbots to improve their performance over time, leading to more accurate and relevant interactions with customers.

Social media and sentiment analysis: Social media platforms are a treasure trove of customer insights, and AI plays a crucial role in data to improve marketing and advertising strategies. Machine learning algorithms can analyze social media data, tracking customer sentiment, engagement, and trends to provide valuable insights into consumer preferences and opinions. By monitoring social media conversations, brands can adjust their strategies, accordingly, addressing customer concerns, and capitalizing on emerging trends.

AI-powered sentiment analysis tools also enable brands to keep a strong online presence, proactively addressing issues and fostering positive brand perception, ultimately contributing to long-term success in the digital space.

Here are few other points to consider when it comes to integrating AI in marketing and advertising:

Personalization at scale: Personalization is a critical part of modern marketing and advertising, and AI can take this to the next level by enabling personalization at scale. By analyzing vast amounts of data and understanding individual customer preferences and behaviors, AI can deliver highly targeted and contextualized experiences across various channels, including email, social media, and mobile apps.

Content optimization: Another area where AI can add value is in content optimization. AI-powered tools can analyze various metrics, such as engagement, click-through rates, and conversion rates, to optimize content for maximum impact. By identifying patterns and trends, AI algorithms can suggest changes to content, such as headlines, images, and calls-to-action, which can improve its performance and achieve better results.

Voice search optimization: Increase use of voice assistants, like Amazon Alexa and Google Home, enhancing content for voice search has become increasingly important. AI can help brands optimize their content for voice search by analyzing conversational language patterns and identifying the most relevant and frequently asked questions. By incorporating these insights into their content strategy, brands can improve the chances of appearing in voice search results, ultimately driving more traffic and engagement.

Integrating AI into marketing and advertising efforts can unlock a wealth of benefits, from improved efficiency and cost savings to personalized experiences and optimized content.

As AI technologies continue to evolve, businesses that embrace this transformative trend can gain a competitive edge, delivering exceptional customer experiences and driving long-term growth and success.

II. Using AI for Brands in Public AI Art Generators

Benefits of leveraging AI art generators

In today's fast-paced digital landscape, captivating visuals are more important than ever for brands seeking to stand out in the crowded marketplace. As Artificial Intelligence (AI) continues to make significant advancements, public AI art generators have emerged as a powerful tool for brands to create stunning and unique visual content. This chapter delves into the ways AI art generators can revolutionize the creative process for businesses and examines the benefits they bring to the table.

The benefits of leveraging AI art generators are manifold. For starters, they provide an unparalleled opportunity for creative exploration and idea generation. Brands can render useful AI's potential to generate an array of designs and styles, tapping into a wellspring of inspiration that can be tailored to meet specific branding objectives. The diverse output of AI art generators not only sparks innovation but also enables brands to stay ahead of design trends and develop truly imaginative content that resonates with their target audience.

Moreover, the cost and time efficiency of AI art generators present a compelling advantage for businesses. With the ability to quickly produce high-quality visuals, brands can significantly reduce the time and resources typically needed for content creation. This efficiency not only allows for a nimbler response to market demands but also frees up valuable resources for other strategic initiatives. In short, AI art generators enable brands to optimize their creative processes and achieve a competitive edge in an increasingly visual-driven world.

Risks and considerations

Despite the numerous advantages AI art generators provide, brands must also be aware of the potential risks and challenges that may arise. Careful consideration is essential when utilizing AI-generated content to ensure it aligns with the brand's overall objectives and values.

One concern is the possible loss of brand identity and consistency. While AI-generated content can be diverse and innovative, it may not always adhere to a brand's established identity and messaging. This inconsistency can lead to confusion among target audiences and dilute the brand's core message. To mitigate this risk, brands should carefully curate and review AI-generated visuals, ensuring they maintain a cohesive and consistent brand image across all branded content.

Another important consideration is data privacy. Brands must be vigilant in handling customer data responsibly and securely when using AI art generators, particularly if the generators utilize user data to create personalized visuals.

Compliance with data protection policies, such as the General Data Protection Regulation (GDPR), is essential to protect consumer privacy and avoid potential legal consequences. By adopting a proactive approach to data privacy and security, brands can ensure they fully utilize the potential of AI art generators without compromising customer trust.

A Word About ChatGPT

In an increasingly connected digital landscape, the advent of public forms of ChatGPT has revolutionized the way we communicate and access information. However, as we embrace this innovation, it is crucial to evaluate the potential risks and considerations involved in deploying such platforms. While their capacity to facilitate seamless conversations and provide tailored responses appears promising, concerns of privacy, data security, and the potential for misuse loom large. As we navigate this uncharted territory, it is essential to strike a balance between leveraging the benefits of ChatGPT and safeguarding users' interests, ultimately shaping a responsible and ethical digital ecosystem.

While OpenAI's public ChatGPT can provide valuable assistance in various applications, there are certain reasons why brands may want to exercise caution before using this tool for their business needs:

Limited control over content: ChatGPT, being an AI language model, may generate content that may not always align with a brand's specific style, tone, or messaging. This could lead to potential inconsistencies in brand communication and a diluted brand identity.

Unintended outputs: As with any AI model, ChatGPT may occasionally generate content that is inappropriate, offensive, or politically sensitive. Brands must carefully review and monitor the AI-generated content to avoid reputational damage.

Intellectual property concerns: When using AI-generated content, brands may face questions regarding the ownership of intellectual property rights. It is essential for brands to understand the legal implications of using ChatGPT and ensure they have the necessary rights to the content it generates.

Data privacy and security: If brands use ChatGPT to handle sensitive customer information or generate personalized content, it is imperative that the brands ensure that they are in compliance with data protection regulations, such as GDPR. If a business fails to secure customer data it can lead to legal consequences and damage brand reputation.

Over-reliance on AI: While ChatGPT can be a helpful tool, brands should avoid becoming overly dependent on

AI-generated content. Human creativity and judgment are still essential in crafting authentic, engaging, and emotionally resonant brand communications.

While OpenAI's public ChatGPT offers numerous benefits, brands should weigh these potential drawbacks and exercise caution when using the tool. By carefully monitoring

AI-generated content and maintaining a balance between human creativity and AI assistance, brands can effectively make use of ChatGPT without jeopardizing their brand image and reputation.

Best practices for using AI in branding

The integration of AI into branding initiatives has opened a world of possibilities for businesses to enhance their brand presence and audience engagement. However, to maximize the potential of AI-driven solutions, it is crucial for brands to adopt a strategic approach and adhere to best practices. By implementing effective guidelines and refining AI-generated content, companies can unlock the full potential of AI in their branding efforts while maintaining a consistent brand image. Firstly, establishing guidelines and parameters is essential for ensuring that AI-generated content aligns with a brand's identity and messaging. Brands should set clear expectations, limitations, and criteria for AI-driven output, enabling the technology to work within predefined boundaries. These guidelines may encompass aspects such as tone, style, language, and targeted demographics. By doing so, brands can maintain a cohesive brand experience across all AI-generated content.

Secondly, evaluating and refining AI-generated content is a critical step in optimizing its effectiveness and engagement. Regular reviews and adjustments of AI-generated content can highlight areas for improvement, ensuring the content is in line with the brand's goals and resonates with the target audience. Brands should analyze performance metrics, gather feedback, and iterate on AI-generated content to continually enhance its impact and relevance.

Adopting best practices for using AI in branding can empower brands to uncover AI-driven solutions while safeguarding brand identity and messaging consistency. By establishing clear guidelines and parameters, and continuously evaluating and refining AI-generated content, brands can create a seamless and engaging experience for their audience, ultimately driving growth and success in the ever-evolving digital landscape.

The utilization of AI technologies, such as public AI art generators and ChatGPT, offers brands the potential to revolutionize their creative processes, enhance audience engagement, and stay ahead in the competitive digital landscape. By leveraging the benefits of AI, businesses can unlock new opportunities for creative exploration and streamline their content creation efforts. However, it is crucial to approach these technologies with caution, considering the risks and challenges related to brand identity, data privacy, and content control. By adopting best practices, striking a balance between human creativity and AI assistance, and ensuring responsible and ethical use of AI-driven solutions, brands can use AI while maintaining a strong and consistent brand image, ultimately propelling them toward success in an ever-evolving digital world.

CHOOSE
GATHER
GENERATE
TRAIN
EVALUATE
DEPLOY
MONITOR

Start Using Generative AI with a Process

Implementing this innovative technology is no simple task, necessitating a multi-stage journey that propels brands toward a future replete with unprecedented opportunities.

This remarkable journey involves the diligent assembly of diverse data for training, judicious selection of an Algorithm, fastidious nurture of the model, meticulous generation and evaluation of outputs, before finally diving into deployment and continuous performance monitoring.

Gather Data: Embarking on the AI journey begins with aggregating diverse input data - text, audio, imagery, or video-that the generative AI model assimilates. Abundant, relevant data propels the model toward producing more realistic and precise outcomes.

Choose an Algorithm: An assortment of unique, power-packed generative AI algorithms are at your disposal, each boasting its strengths and accommodating certain weaknesses. Brands should discerningly opt for an algorithm that aligns with their specific requirements.

Train Model: Having selected a fitting algorithm, it's time to train the model on your data reservoir. Brace for an exhaustive duration, as this phase hinges upon your data volume and the complexity of the algorithm.

Generate Outputs: A trained model is ready to showcase its potential by creating outputs. Activate this process by providing it with a data set and guiding it to yield results akin to the set.

Evaluate Outputs: It is crucial to appraise the outputs delivered by the generative AI model, ensuring they adhere to the quality standards. This evaluation can be undertaken through manual inspection or leveraging automated tools.

Deploy Model: A successful evaluation heralds the moment for the model's deployment, making it accessible for users to generate outputs.

Monitor Results: Post-deployment, consistent monitoring of the model's performance is vital, examining the volume and quality of produced outputs, and incorporating user feedback.

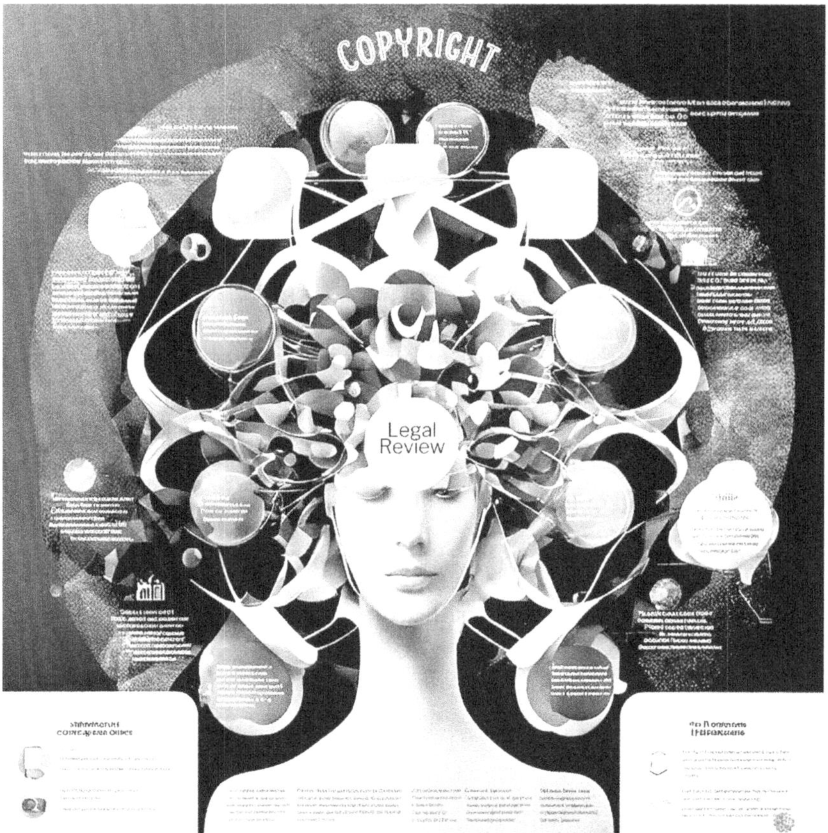
COPYRIGHT
Legal
Review

III. Copyright and AI

Intellectual Property Rights

As artificial intelligence is quickly advancing, the landscape of intellectual property rights has become increasingly complex and uncertain. As AI-generated content gains prominence, the question of ownership and the application of traditional copyright laws have left many grappling to find answers. This article will delve into the ongoing debates surrounding AI-generated content ownership, the legal precedents at play, and the challenges businesses must navigate to protect their brand assets and copyright while fostering innovation and collaboration in the world of AI.

Who owns AI-generated content?

As AI-generated content continues to proliferate, questions surrounding its ownership and intellectual property rights have become a pressing concern. Traditionally, copyright law has been designed to protect the creative works of human authors. However, with AI-generated content, it is unclear whether the AI system, its developer, or the end-user should be considered the legal owner. The answer remains a subject of ongoing debate, with different jurisdictions adopting different approaches to this complex issue.

Legal precedents and ongoing debates

Legal precedents regarding AI-generated content ownership is currently limited, as the nature of AI technology continually presents new challenges. Some jurisdictions, like the United States, have taken the stance that AI-generated works are not eligible for copyright protection, as they are not created by a human author. Conversely, other jurisdictions, such as the European Union, have proposed extending certain intellectual property rights to AI-generated content. The debate is far from settled, and it is crucial for brands to actively monitor developments in this area to protect their interests.

Protecting brand assets and copyright

Monitoring unauthorized use of brand elements. As the use of AI becomes more widespread, brands must be vigilant in monitoring and protecting their intellectual property. This includes keeping an eye on AI-generated content that may infringe on their copyrights or misappropriate their brand elements. Tools such as reverse image search engines and AI-driven content monitoring software can help brands detect unauthorized usage and take swift action to protect their assets.

Legal recourse and enforcement

If a brand discovers unauthorized use of its copyrighted material or brand elements in AI-generated content, it is essential to act quickly and decisively. The business may send out cease and desist letters, initiating legal proceedings, or collaborating with AI developers and platforms to address the issue. Brands should consult with legal experts to determine the most effective course of action based on their specific circumstances. Navigating legal challenges and ethical considerations

Balancing innovation with legal compliance

Brands must strike a delicate balance between embracing the innovative potential of AI-generated content and adhering to intellectual property laws. This involves staying informed about the evolving legal landscape and adjusting their strategies accordingly. Brands should establish clear guidelines for their use of AI-generated content to ensure they are operating within the confines of the law while still pushing the boundaries of what is possible with AI technology.

Collaborating with AI developers and platforms

To navigate the complex legal and ethical challenges surrounding AI-generated content, brands should actively collaborate with AI developers and platforms. This partnership can help ensure that AI-generated content aligns with the brand's values, respects intellectual property rights, and conforms to relevant laws and regulations. By working together, brands and AI developers can forge a path forward that promotes innovation and protecting the rights and interests of all parties involved.

The intersection of AI-generated content and intellectual property rights remains a dynamic and evolving area of concern. As legal frameworks and ethical considerations continue to be challenged by AI advancements, businesses must remain vigilant in protecting their interests while embracing the potential of this groundbreaking technology. By actively monitoring legal developments, forging collaborative partnerships with AI developers and platforms, and maintaining a delicate balance between innovation and compliance, businesses can navigate the complex terrain of

AI-generated content ownership and forge a path that benefits all stakeholders in this ever-changing digital landscape.

IV. Case Studies: Brands Successfully Using AI

The integration of artificial intelligence (AI) has emerged as a game-changer for brands across various industries. From streaming services to beauty retailers, companies are leveraging AI to revolutionize their branding and marketing strategies. By leveraging the power of AI algorithms and technologies, these brands are unlocking new levels of personalization, customer engagement, and data-driven decision-making. In this chapter, we will explore some of the successful implementations of AI by notable brands and delve into the lessons learned and best practices they have adopted. Furthermore, we will take a glimpse into the future, examining the expanding role of AI in branding and marketing and the ethical considerations that come with it.

Numerous brands across various industries have embraced AI to enhance their branding and marketing efforts. Some notable examples include:

Netflix: The streaming giant uses AI-powered algorithms to analyze user behavior and preferences, allowing them to provide personalized recommendations and enhance user experience.

Coca-Cola: Revolutionizing the brand experience with the aid of AI technology, Coca-Cola teamed up with Bain & Company and OpenAI developing cutting-edge marketing and consumer experience solutions. Generative AI algorithms can quickly create text, images and other content in the brand image of Coca-Cola.

Sephora: The beauty retailer has integrated AI-powered virtual try-on tools and personalized product recommendations, creating a seamless and engaging customer experience.

Nestle: In a brilliant venture, Ogilvy showcased the innovational prowess of AI in advertising with a campaign for Nestlé's The Milkmaid yogurt, designed for the French market. Prompted by the media attention surrounding Vermeer's esteemed painting, The Milkmaid, when new details were uncovered via X-ray, Ogilvy seized this opportunity. Utilizing the generative AI tool, DALL-E 2, and produced imaginative extensions of the original canvas that resonated with the renewed interest in the artwork. This clever harnessing of the AI-generated video's viral nature allowed the brand to gain significant visibility, tapping into the cultural momentum with zero media spend. An inspiring example of how AI can catalyze marketing strategies, turning cultural insights into branding opportunities and maximizing return on investment without any additional spend.

Wendy's: In a visionary move, Wendy's has joined forces with Google, to revolutionize the ordering process in quick-service restaurants (QSR) with the introduction of FreshAI. This AI-driven chatbot, deployed at Wendy's drive-thrus, is an exemplar of the transformative potential of AI in the QSR industry. Initially conceived to enhance the customer experience by boosting speed, improving accuracy, and ensuring consistent service at drive-thrus, FreshAI underscores the notion that AI is not just an emerging technology but a catalyst for innovation and accelerated growth in today's highly competitive market. It is a testament to the exciting possibilities that lie ahead at the junction of AI, branding, and marketing.

Lessons Learned

Beside a mindset of openness, Brands that have successfully implemented AI share some common lessons and best practices:

Prioritize customer experience: Successful AI integration should enhance the customer experience, offering personalized and relevant content, products, or services.

Collaborate with AI experts: Partnering with AI developers or platforms can ensure a smooth implementation process, tailored to the brand's specific needs and goals.

Continuously monitor and refine AI solutions: Brands should regularly assess the effectiveness of AI-driven initiatives, making adjustments as needed to optimize results.

Maintain brand consistency: While leveraging AI-generated content, brands must ensure that it aligns with their established identity and messaging to maintain a consistent brand image.

The future of AI in branding and marketing

As AI technology continues to advance, its role in branding and marketing is expected to grow.

More personalized experiences: AI will enable brands to deliver increasingly tailored content and experiences, catering to each customer's unique preferences and needs.

Enhanced creativity: AI-generated content will become more sophisticated, pushing the boundaries of creativity and providing brands with new ways to engage their audiences.

Improved data-driven decision-making: AI-powered analytics will provide brands with deeper insights into customer behavior and market trends, informing more effective strategies and decisions.

Ethical considerations: As AI becomes more integrated into branding and marketing, brands will need to navigate the ethical implications of AI-generated content, data privacy, and intellectual property rights. By staying informed and adaptable, brands can use AI to drive innovation, enhance customer experiences, and achieve lasting success in the evolving world of marketing and branding.

As we look ahead, the future of branding and marketing appears intertwined with the continued advancements in AI technology. The potential for personalized experiences, enhanced creativity, and data-driven decision-making is boundless. However, with great power comes great responsibility, and brands must navigate the ethical considerations that arise as AI becomes more deeply integrated into their strategies. By prioritizing the customer experience, collaborating with AI experts, continuously monitoring and refining AI solutions, and maintaining brand consistency, companies can pave the way for success in this new era. As the landscape evolves, staying informed and adaptable will be essential for brands to take advantage of the full potential of AI, drive innovation, and achieve lasting success in the ever-changing world of marketing and branding.

BEST
PRACTICES

V. Best Practices for Brands Using AI Services

In the fast-paced and ever-changing world of technology, integrating Artificial Intelligence (AI) into branding and marketing strategies has become imperative for businesses aiming to stay ahead of the competition. Section VI delves into the optimal approaches for brands aiming to leverage the potential of AI. This section emphasizes the importance of selecting appropriate AI solutions and partners, evaluating AI platforms and service providers, and choosing the ideal AI platform or service provider for seamless integration and to maximize the influence on your brand's growth and achievement.

Choosing the right AI solutions and partners

Selecting the right AI solutions and partners is of paramount importance for businesses and brands. These decisions directly impact the business and brand's ability to stay competitive, optimize operations, and deliver a personalized and engaging customer experience. By aligning with the most suitable AI solution and partner, businesses can fully make use of AI, enabling them to make data-driven decisions, automate processes, and uncover valuable insights that drive innovation and growth.

Furthermore, the right AI partner can provide invaluable expertise and support throughout the integration process, ensuring a fluid transition, and maximizing the return on investment.

Evaluating AI platforms and service providers is a critical step in ensuring that the selected AI solution aligns with a brand's unique needs and goals. By thoroughly assessing the capabilities, features, and scalability of various AI platforms and service providers, businesses can identify the most appropriate solution that complements their existing processes and objectives. This helps in streamlining operations, improving customer engagement, and driving innovation tailored to the brand's vision. Moreover, a well-aligned AI solution fosters a more efficient and effective utilization of resources, ultimately contributing to the brand's long-term success and sustainability in an increasingly competitive market.

Evaluating AI Readiness

Is Your Brand Ready to Embrace the Power of AI? AI technology is rapidly becoming an essential driver of innovation and growth in the realm of branding and marketing. Skyrocket has expertly crafted a platform that enables your business to seamlessly transition into the world of AI readiness. By assessing your brand's unique strengths and opportunities, to utilize AI's tremendous potential to revolutionize the way you engage with your audience. As a forward-thinking marketer, recognizing the importance of staying informed and adaptable is crucial to unlocking unparalleled opportunities and keeping a competitive edge in the market.

In considering your brand's readiness to incorporate AI technology, there are five essential inquiries to consider:

1. What are the specific challenges your brand aims to address with AI? Pinpointing these clear objectives will steer the AI integration in an intentional and relevant direction.

2. What internal and external data resources does the brand have at its disposal to tackle these challenges? The quality, quantity, and pertinence of available data can significantly affect the efficacy of AI algorithms.

3. Can your existing technological framework

adequately support an AI transition? A rigorous evaluation of existing technology systems and their capability to accommodate necessary AI equipment and resources is critical for successful integration.

4. Does your team possess the fundamental skill sets to adeptly develop, implement, and manage AI operations? An assessment of your team's core competencies and understanding pertaining to AI will determine your readiness for adopting AI.

5. How open is your organization to AI-led transformation? Examining the openness and adaptability of a company's prevailing culture to change can decide the feasibility of a successful AI integration.

Discerning the answers to these questions will markedly enhance your understanding of brand readiness for AI and will facilitate a strategic pathway toward AI adoption.

Assessing platforms and service providers

Selecting the most suitable AI platform or service provider is crucial to successfully integrating AI into your branding and marketing strategy. When evaluating potential partners, brands should consider the following factors:

- **Track record**: Look for AI platforms or

service providers with a proven record of success, demonstrated through case studies, testimonials, and client references. Technological capabilities: Assess the sophistication and effectiveness of the AI technology offered, ensuring it aligns with your brand's specific requirements.

- **Customization and scalability**: Opt for solutions that are adaptable to your brand's needs and can scale as your business grows.

- **Support and collaboration**: Choose partners that offer comprehensive support and are willing to collaborate closely with your brand throughout the AI integration process.

Aligning AI capabilities with brand needs and goals

To ensure the successful integration of AI into your branding and marketing efforts, it is essential to align AI capabilities with your brand's specific needs and objectives:

- **Define clear goals**: Identify the primary objectives you wish to achieve through AI integration, such as improved customer engagement, increased sales, or more effective marketing campaigns.

- **Assess your resources**: Determine your brand's existing resources, both in terms of personnel and technological infrastructure, and consider how AI can complement and enhance these resources.

- **Identify areas of improvement**: Pinpoint aspects of your branding and marketing strategy that could benefit from AI-driven solutions, such as personalized content creation, customer service automation, or data-driven decision-making.

- **Consider potential challenges**: Be aware of potential obstacles or limitations, such as data privacy concerns, intellectual property rights, or ethical implications, and seek AI solutions that address these challenges.

By carefully evaluating AI platforms and service providers and aligning AI capabilities with your brand's needs and goals, you can successfully implement AI-driven solutions that drive innovation and enhance your branding and marketing efforts.

Integrating AI into existing brand workflows

Collaboration between human and AI teams

Successfully integrating AI into your brand workflows requires seamless collaboration between human and AI teams. This can be achieved by:

- Establishing clear roles: Define the specific responsibilities of both human and AI teams, ensuring that each member understands their function in the overall workflow.

- Open communication: Inspire a culture to embrace open communication between human and AI teams, encouraging feedback, questions, and suggestions to optimize the AI integration process.

- Training and education: Provide human team members with the necessary training and resources to effectively collaborate with AI-driven tools and platforms, ensuring they are comfortable with the technology and can maximize its potential.

- Regular progress evaluations: Conduct periodic assessments of the collaboration between human and AI teams, identifying any areas that require improvement and implementing necessary changes.

Adapting and updating processes to accommodate AI

As AI becomes an integral part of your brand workflows, it's essential to adapt and update existing processes to accommodate the technology:

- Process mapping: Identify and map out current workflows, noting areas where AI can be integrated to streamline tasks, enhance efficiency, or improve results.

- Implementing AI step-by-step: Introduce AI-driven solutions gradually, focusing on one area or process at a time, allowing for easier adaptation and minimizing potential disruptions.

- Continual optimization: Regularly evaluate and refine AI-integrated processes, using data and feedback to adjust as needed to ensure optimal performance.

- Embracing change: Inspire your team to embrace change and view AI integration as an opportunity for growth and improvement, fostering a mindset of adaptability and innovation.

By fostering collaboration between human and AI teams and adapting existing processes to accommodate AI, brands can seamlessly integrate AI-driven solutions into their workflows, ultimately enhancing their marketing and branding efforts.

Ensuring Data Privacy and Security

In the era of AI-driven solutions, data privacy and security have become increasingly important for brands to retain customer trust and comply with regulatory requirements.

This section highlights the significance of responsible data collection and usage practices, as well as the need for compliance with data protection regulations. Additionally, it emphasizes the importance of monitoring and measuring AI performance to optimize results and maximize the benefits of AI integration, while fostering a culture of innovation and experimentation to support continuous growth and adaptation in the dynamic world of AI.

Responsible data collection and usage

As AI-driven solutions rely heavily on data, it is critical for brands to ensure responsible data collection and usage practices:

Obtain consent: Collect data only from individuals who have provided their explicit consent, clearly informing them of the purpose and scope of data collection.

- Limit data collection: Collect only the data that is necessary to achieve specific goals, avoiding excessive or irrelevant data collection.

- Secure storage and handling: Implement robust security measures to protect stored data and ensure it is handled securely throughout the data processing lifecycle.

- Data anonymization: Use anonymization techniques to remove personally identifiable information (PII) from collected data, reducing the risk of privacy breaches.

Compliance with data protection regulations

Brands must also ensure compliance with data protection laws and regulations. Refer to the General Data Protection Regulation (GDPR) in the European Union and the California Consumer Privacy Act (CCPA) in the United States:

- Understand the regulations: Familiarize yourself with the data protection laws and regulations applicable to your brand, ensuring you are aware of your obligations and requirements.

- Designate a data protection officer (DPO): Appoint a DPO who is responsible for supervising data protection compliance and ensuring best practices are followed.

- Implement privacy-by-design principles: Integrate data protection measures into the design and development of AI-driven solutions, proactively addressing potential privacy issues.

- Regular audits and assessments: Conduct periodic audits and assessments of your data protection practices and AI-driven solutions, ensuring ongoing compliance and identifying areas for improvement.

By prioritizing data privacy and security and ensuring compliance with data protection regulations, brands can develop trust with their customers, and mitigate the risks associated with data-driven AI solutions.

Monitoring and measuring AI performance

Monitoring and measuring AI performance, delves into the importance of establishing key performance indicators (KPIs) for AI initiatives and continuously refining AI solutions based on data-driven insights to optimize results and maximize the benefits of AI integration.

Setting key performance indicators (KPIs) for AI initiatives To effectively evaluate the success of AI-driven solutions, brands must establish clear and measurable key performance indicators (KPIs) for their AI initiatives:

- Align KPIs with objectives: Ensure that the KPIs you choose align with the specific goals you aim to achieve through AI integration, such as increased sales, higher customer satisfaction, or improved marketing ROI.

- Quantifiable metrics: Select KPIs that can be quantified and tracked over time, allowing for objective measurement of AI performance.

- Set benchmarks: Establish baseline performance levels for each KPI, providing a point of comparison to gauge the impact of

AI-driven solutions.

- Balance short-term and long-term metrics: Combine short-term KPIs that measure immediate results with long-term KPIs that track the enduring impact of AI integration on your brand's overall performance.

Continuously refining AI solutions based on performance insights monitoring and measuring AI performance allows brands to make data-driven decisions and continuously refine their AI-driven solutions:

- Analyze performance data: Regularly review AI performance data, identifying trends, patterns, and areas of success or underperformance.

- Adjust AI strategies: Based on performance insights, make adjustments to your AI strategy, fine-tuning algorithms, processes, or workflows as needed to improve results.

- Test and iterate: Experiment with different AI-driven solutions, comparing their performance against established KPIs to identify the most effective approaches for your brand.

Cultivate an ethos of continuous improvement: Encourage your team to view AI performance monitoring and refinement as an ongoing process, ensuring that your brand continually adapts and evolves to stay ahead of the curve.

By setting clear KPIs for AI initiatives and continuously refining AI solutions based on performance insights, brands can optimize their AI-driven strategies and maximize the benefits of AI integration.

Fostering a culture of innovation and experimentation

Fostering a culture of innovation and experimentation is essential for organizations to fully capitalize on AI-driven solutions, enabling them to encourage creativity, risk-taking, and continuous improvement while embracing AI as a powerful tool for growth.

Encouraging creativity and risk-taking

To unleash the full potential of AI-driven solutions, brands must encourage innovation and experimentation by:

- Empowering employees: Provide a supportive environment where employees feel encouraged to think creatively, take risks, and explore new approaches to problem-solving.

- Celebrating failures as learning opportunities: Embrace failures as valuable sources of insight, helping your team understand that setbacks can pave the way for future successes.

- Promoting cross-functional collaboration: Encourage teams from different departments to work together, combining their diverse skill sets and perspectives to fuel innovation.

Offering ongoing training and development: Invest in the continuous growth of your employees, providing them with the necessary resources and opportunities to expand their knowledge and skill set.

Embracing AI as a tool for continuous improvement and growth

To fully benefit from the capability of AI, brands should view it as a catalyst for continuous improvement and growth:

- Adopt a growth mindset: Encourage your team to see AI as an opportunity to learn, grow, and adapt, rather than as a threat to existing roles or processes.

- Integrate AI throughout the organization: Leverage AI-driven solutions across various departments and functions, promoting a shared understanding of its capabilities and potential impact.

- Stay up to date with AI advancements: Keep abreast of the latest changes in AI technology, make certain your brand remains at the forefront of innovation.

- Encourage knowledge sharing: Inspire openness and transparency, where team members are encouraged to share their AI-related learnings, successes, and challenges, creating a collective pool of knowledge and experience.

Brands can unlock new opportunities, drive efficiency, and stay ahead in the competitive landscape through fostering a culture of innovation and experimentation and embracing AI as a tool for continuous improvement and growth,

OPEN
ALL

VI. Public vs. Embedded AI Training for Brands

Brands are increasingly discovering the potential of artificial intelligence to optimize their operations, enhance customer experiences, and drive innovation. A critical component of successful AI integration lies in effective training, which can be broadly categorized into two approaches: Public AI Training and Embedded AI Training. As brands strive to make informed decisions regarding their AI strategies, it is crucial to understand the nuances, benefits, and potential drawbacks of these two training methodologies. This section will explore Public vs. Embedded AI Training, providing insights into their core differences and guiding brands to make informed choices that best align with their objectives and organizational needs.

Understanding the differences

Public AI training: Accessible AI platforms and services

Public AI training involves leveraging pre-built AI models and tools offered by accessible platforms and services, such as

Google's TensorFlow, Microsoft's Azure, or Amazon's AWS. These platforms provide a range of AI solutions that cater to diverse use cases, from chatbots and recommendation engines to data analysis and automation. The primary advantages of public AI training include:

- Cost-effectiveness: By utilizing existing resources and infrastructure, public AI training can be a more affordable option for brands, particularly for those with limited budgets or resources.

- Ease of implementation: Public AI platforms and services typically offer user-friendly interfaces and documentation, enabling brands to integrate AI solutions quickly and easily into their existing systems.

- Scalability: As these platforms are designed to cater to a wide range of businesses and applications, they often offer scalable solutions that can grow alongside a brand's needs.

Embedded AI training: Custom-built AI solutions

In contrast, embedded AI training refers to the development of bespoke AI models and algorithms tailored specifically to a brand's unique requirements and objectives. This approach allows for a higher degree of customization and control, as brands can design AI solutions that address specific challenges or capitalize on unique opportunities. Key benefits of embedded AI training include:

- **Tailored solutions**: Custom-built AI models can be designed to address specific pain points or opportunities, ensuring a more focused and effective impact on a brand's operations and goals.
- **Competitive advantage**: As embedded AI solutions are tailored to a brand's specific needs, they can offer a competitive edge that is difficult for rivals to replicate.
- **Enhanced data security**: Developing in-house AI solutions can provide greater control over data privacy and security, particularly in industries where sensitive data is involved.

By understanding the differences between public and embedded AI training, brands can make informed decisions about which approach best aligns with their objectives, resources, and overall AI strategy.

Evaluating the benefits and drawbacks

Cost considerations and resource allocation

When deciding between public AI training and embedded AI training, brands must carefully consider the costs involved and the resources required for each approach. Public AI training can be more cost-effective due to the use of existing platforms and infrastructure; however, subscription fees and usage costs can add up over time. On the other hand, embedded AI training requires a greater initial investment in the development of custom solutions but can lead to long-term cost savings as brands do not need to rely on external services.

Flexibility and adaptability to brand needs

Another critical factor to consider is the flexibility and adaptability of each AI training approach. Public AI platforms offer a range of pre-built solutions that can be quickly implemented and scaled; however, they may not always cater to specific brand needs or offer the desired level of customization. Embedded AI training provides greater flexibility by allowing brands to develop tailored solutions that address their unique challenges and opportunities. This approach, however, may require a more significant investment of time and resources, and may not be as easily scalable as public AI platforms.

Data privacy and security concerns

Data privacy and security are important concerns for brands when implementing AI solutions. Public AI platforms often have robust security measures in place, but using external services can still pose risks to data privacy. Furthermore, some platforms may require data sharing or storage on third-party servers, which can create additional security concerns. Embedded AI training can offer better control over data privacy and security, as brands can develop and manage their AI solutions in-house. However, this approach may require the development of additional security measures and protocols to ensure the protection of sensitive data.

In conclusion, when evaluating the benefits and drawbacks of public AI training and embedded AI training, brands must consider factors such as cost, flexibility, adaptability, and data privacy and security. By carefully assessing these factors, organizations can make informed decisions about which approach will best support their AI strategies and deliver the desired outcomes.

Selecting the appropriate approach for your brand Assessing current and future brand objectives

To determine the best AI training approach for your brand, it is crucial to carefully assess your current and future objectives. Begin by identifying the key challenges your organization faces and the specific goals you aim to achieve through AI integration. Consider both short-term and long-term objectives, as well as potential changes in your industry landscape that may impact your AI strategy. By aligning your AI training approach with your brand objectives, you can ensure that your investment in AI delivers the desired results and contributes to your overall business success.

Balancing efficiency, customization, and control

Another essential aspect in selecting the appropriate AI training approach is striking a balance between efficiency, customization, and control. Public AI training can offer a more efficient solution that allows for rapid implementation and scalability but may lack the desired level of customization and control. Embedded AI training, on the other hand, provides greater customization and control but may require more time and resources to develop and maintain. Weigh the importance of these factors against your brand objectives and resources to determine which approach will best serve your needs.

Selecting the appropriate AI training approach for your brand requires a thorough understanding of your objectives, as well as a careful evaluation of the balance between efficiency, customization, and control. By considering these factors and aligning your AI strategy with your overall brand goals, you can select the best approach that will drive growth, innovation, and competitive advantage in today's ever-evolving digital landscape. Strategies for successful implementation

Collaborating with AI developers and partners

A critical component of successfully implementing an AI training approach is establishing strong collaboration between your brand and AI developers or partners. This collaboration can involve working with in-house development teams, external AI experts, or both, as needed. Effective communication, knowledge sharing, and alignment of goals and expectations are essential to ensure that your AI solutions are designed, developed, and deployed in a manner that meets your brand's unique requirements and objectives. By fostering a collaborative environment, your organization can benefit from shared expertise and insights, ultimately driving innovation and growth.

Continuously refining and optimizing AI training models

Another important strategy for successful implementation is the continuous refinement and optimization of your AI training models. As your brand evolves and grows, it is crucial to ensure that your AI solutions remain effective and relevant.

Regularly review your AI models' performance and make adjustments as necessary to account for changes in your business needs, industry trends, or technological advancements. This process of continual improvement will enable your AI solutions to adapt and deliver optimal results over time, ensuring long-term success and sustainability.

Ensuring seamless integration with brand strategy and operations

Finally, it is essential to ensure that your chosen AI training approach is seamlessly integrated with your overall brand strategy and operations. This integration involves not only the technical aspects of implementing AI solutions but also the alignment of your AI strategy with your brand's goals, values, and culture. Educate and train your team members on the use of AI and its potential impact on their roles and responsibilities. Encourage open dialogue and collaboration between AI developers and other stakeholders within your organization to foster a shared understanding of how AI can drive growth and success.

Implementing a successful AI training approach requires collaboration with AI developers and partners, continuous refinement and optimization of AI models, and seamless integration with your brand strategy and operations. By focusing on these strategies, your organization can maximize the potential of AI and unlock new opportunities for growth, innovation, and competitive advantage.

Successful implementation of AI in branding and marketing strategies require a comprehensive approach that encompasses various best practices. Brands should prioritize educating employees on the potential of AI and its applications, setting clear policies and guidelines for AI integration, and creating strategic plans that align with their business objectives. Monitoring and measuring AI performance is essential for continuous optimization and maximizing its benefits. Furthermore, fostering a culture that encourages creativity, risk-taking, and innovation will help brands embrace AI as a powerful tool for continuous improvement and growth. By adopting these best practices, brands can effectively leverage AI to drive success in today's competitive market.

Here are five steps a brand should take to get started with using AI

1. Know your goal: Clearly define the objectives you aim to achieve through AI integration, such as improving customer experience or streamlining operations.

2. Get educated and involved: Familiarize your team with AI capabilities and involve them in the process, as they are in the best position to judge the effectiveness of AI in their workflows.

3. Start small and scale: Begin with a small AI project, evaluate its performance, gather user feedback, and then scale AI capabilities to other processes and use cases.

4. Implement privacy-by-design principles: Integrate data protection measures into the design and development of AI-driven solutions, proactively addressing potential privacy issues.

5. Inspire exploration and experimentation: Encourage creativity, risk-taking, and continuous improvement within your organization, ensuring that your brand continually adapts and evolves to stay ahead of the curve.

LET'S GO!

VII. Let's Go!

Embracing the AI Revolution in Branding and Marketing

As we embark on a new era of digital transformation, the world of branding and marketing is undergoing a paradigm shift. Artificial Intelligence (AI) has emerged as a

game-changing force, offering brands the ability to create more personalized, engaging, and effective marketing campaigns than ever before. But as we dive headfirst into this exciting new frontier, it's essential to approach AI with a blend of enthusiasm and caution, ensuring that we use its potential responsibly and sustainably. In this section, we will explore the ongoing evolution of AI and its impact on brands, discuss strategies for preparing for the future of AI in branding and marketing, and examine how organizations can embrace AI as a tool for growth and innovation while maintaining ethical practices and customer trust. So, without further ado, let's go!

The ongoing evolution of AI and its impact on brands

The rapid development of AI technologies is transforming the world of branding and marketing in ways that were once unimaginable. From personalized customer experiences to data-driven decision-making, AI is revolutionizing how brands connect with their audiences and stay ahead of the competition. However, with great power comes great responsibility. As AI continues to evolve, brands must be cautious in their approach, ensuring that they strike the right balance between leveraging AI's potential and maintaining trust with their customers.

Preparing for the future of AI in branding and marketing

To stay ahead of the competitors, brands must be proactive in preparing for the future of AI in branding and marketing. This involves carefully evaluating the benefits and drawbacks of different AI training approaches, such as public AI training and embedded AI training. By considering factors like cost, flexibility, adaptability, and data privacy and security, brands can make informed decisions about which approach will best support their AI strategies and deliver the desired outcomes.

But beware! While AI offers numerous opportunities for growth and innovation, it also presents potential pitfalls. Brands must be vigilant in ensuring that their AI strategies align with their core values, and that they maintain transparency and ethical practices in their use of AI technologies.

Embracing AI as a tool for growth and innovation

Using AI's power for growth and innovation requires a commitment to ongoing improvement and integration. By fostering collaboration with AI developers and partners, continuously refining and optimizing AI models, and ensuring seamless integration with brand strategy and operations, businesses can take advantage of AI's full potential. In doing so, they position themselves for growth, innovation, and competitive advantage.

But remember, with great power comes great responsibility. As brands embrace AI, they must also be careful of the potential risks and challenges associated with its use. By staying informed, agile, and proactive in their AI strategies, brands can use AI to revolutionize their marketing efforts, drive customer engagement, and propel their businesses forward into a future where AI plays an essential role in their success.

Keep in Mind

The ongoing evolution of AI is reshaping the future of branding and marketing, presenting both exciting opportunities and potential challenges for businesses. By staying informed, agile, and proactive in their AI strategies, brands can navigate the ever-changing AI landscape to drive growth, innovation, and competitive advantage. But, as we venture into this brave new world, let's not forget the importance of maintaining trust and ethical practices, ensuring that our pursuit of AI-driven success is both responsible and sustainable.

Utilizing Generative AI for Brand Advancement

Generative AI serves as a dynamic and evolving tool, offering brands innovative ways to stand out competitively. Among the emerging trends and specific applications of generative AI within brand development are:

Personalized Content

Generative AI enables brands to create bespoke content tailored to individual customers. Functions include:

Personalized product recommendations: AI-driven suggestions based on user preferences, browsing habits, and purchase history, promoting relevant items to each customer. Tailored marketing messages: Customized communication specific to customer interests and behavior patterns, ensuring more effective engagement.

Custom-generated images or videos: Unique visual content conceived by analyzing user preferences and data, capturing the attention of target audiences.

Example: Nike utilizes generative AI in devising personalized product recommendations for clients. The company's AI system assesses customer data to discern preferences before suggesting relevant products, leading to heightened customer engagement and sales.

Automated Creative Workflows

By automating creative workflows, generative AI allows human designers more time to concentrate on strategic tasks. Applications involve:

Generating new product ideas: Leverage AI to examine current trends, user preferences, and industry data, driving innovation and ideation in product development.

Crafting marketing campaigns: Automate the design of marketing materials and creative assets based on user preferences, engagement metrics, and company-specific branding guidelines.

Developing unique branding assets: Use AI-generated content, such as logos, fonts, and color schemes, to create a distinctive brand identity.

Example: H&M applies generative AI to conceive innovative clothing products. The company's AI system produces new designs, synthesized from current trends and consumer preferences, resulting in cutting-edge and captivating products that save time and resources.

Enhanced Customer Experiences

Generative AI enriches customer experiences across a range of aspects. This includes:

Delivering personalized customer service: Leverage AI conversational agents and chatbots to provide swift, context-based support tailored to individuals' needs and interests.

Constructing engaging product pages: Automated generation of enticing product images, videos, and descriptions according to user preferences, leading to higher user engagement and conversion rates.

Establishing novel methods for customer-brand interaction: Innovate interactive experiences, such as voice-activated assistants, AR/VR applications, and enriched user interfaces, to deepen brand-client relationships.

Example: Pinterest employs generative AI to create more captivating product pages. By generating new images and videos, the company's AI system increases visibility, translating to higher click-through rates and sales.

GET BEADY TO
BLAST OFE

VIII. Getting Started

Here are five important frameworks a brand needs to use with working with generative AI:

By following these frameworks, brands can ensure that they are using generative AI in a responsible and effective way.

These questions will help brands judge the business readiness for using generative AI.

Strategic Fit

Brands need to ensure that generative AI is used in a way that aligns with their overall business goals and objectives. For example, if a brand is looking to improve customer experience, they could use generative AI to create personalized recommendations or generate creative product descriptions.

> Will the usage of generative AI help this brand reach its objective?
>
> Does generative AI use align with the overall strategy of the brand?
>
> What are risks associated with using generative AI?

Does the brand have the resources to adequately ensure the data is secure?

What are the potential benefits of using generative AI?

How will the implementation of generative AI affect customers?

Are there any potential legal or compliance issues with generative AI use?

Can the brand afford the cost associated with using generative AI?

Will the output of generative AI meet brand requirements?

How will the brand measure the success of the generative AI use?

Functional Feasibility

Brands need to consider whether the use case they are considering is technically feasible with current generative AI capabilities. For example, if a brand wants to use generative AI to create realistic-looking images, they will need to make sure that they have access to a large enough dataset of images to train the AI model.

Does the brand have access to the necessary data for training the AI model?

Are there any technical limitations with the existing generative AI capabilities?

Will the generative AI be able to solve the given use case?

Are there any existing tools or code that can be leveraged to reduce the effort needed to implement the generative AI?

Does the brand have the necessary resources to develop and deploy the generative AI?

Are there any performance issues that could arise from using generative AI?

Is the generative AI suitable for the intended application environment?

How long will it take to implement the generative AI?

Is the brand equipped to handle any unexpected results from the generative AI?

Are there any risks associated with using generative AI for the given use case?

Technical Feasibility

Brands need to ensure that they have the technical infrastructure in place to support the use of generative AI. This includes having access to a powerful computer or server, as well as the necessary software and libraries.

Does the brand have access to a powerful computer or server to support the use of generative AI?

Do any additional software or libraries need to be installed before generative AI can be implemented?

Is the brand's existing IT infrastructure compatible with generative AI?

Does the brand have the necessary expertise to set up and maintain the generative AI systems?

Has the necessary training been done to ensure staff are familiar with generative AI?

Are there any additional hardware, software, or services needed to deploy generative AI?

Are there any potential risks associated with using generative AI?

Is the generative AI suitable for the intended application environment?

How long will it take to set up the generative AI infrastructure?

Are there any legal or compliance concerns with using generative AI for the given use case?

Risks and Benefits

Brands need to carefully consider the risks and benefits of using generative AI. For example, one risk is that generative AI could be used to generate fake or misleading content.

However, the benefits of using generative AI can be significant, such as the ability to create new and innovative marketing campaigns.

What are the potential risks associated with using generative AI for the given purpose?

What are the potential benefits of incorporating generative AI in the brand's strategy?

Is there a potential for legal or ethical concerns related to using generative AI?

Will the brand be able to measure the results of incorporating generative AI?

What is the likelihood that the brand may incur financial losses from using generative AI?

What actions are necessary to mitigate the risks involved in using generative AI?

Are there any potential long-term impacts of using generative AI?

Does the brand have the resources and expertise to effectively implement and manage generative AI?

Are there any potential competitive advantages from using generative AI?

How will customers be impacted by incorporating generative AI into the brand's strategy?

Human Oversight

Brands need to ensure that there is human oversight of generative AI systems. This means that humans need to be involved in the process of creating and reviewing the content that is generated by AI models. This helps to ensure that the content is accurate, safe, and compliant with all relevant regulations.

Does the team have the necessary expertise to oversee generative AI systems?

Are there any existing policies and procedures related to using generative AI?

Is there a process in place for regularly reviewing the content generated by generative AI?

Are there any potential legal or regulatory issues associated with using generative AI?

Are there guidelines in place to ensure that humans are involved in the process of creating and reviewing content?

What steps are needed to ensure that any generated content is accurate and compliant?

What processes should be implemented to ensure safe and effective use of generative AI?

Are there any potential risks associated with human oversight of generative AI systems?

How will the team measure the success of implementing generative AI systems?

Are there any measures needed to protect customers and their data from potential misuse of generative AI?

Additional considerations for brands using generative AI

Data privacy: Brands need to be aware of the privacy implications of using generative AI. This includes ensuring that they have the necessary consent to collect and use personal data, and that they are taking steps to protect the privacy of individuals.

Bias: Brands need to be aware of the potential for bias in generative AI models. This is because AI models are trained on data that is collected from the real world, and this data can reflect existing biases in society. Brands need to take steps to mitigate bias in their AI models, such as using a diverse dataset for training and using techniques to identify and remove bias from the models.

Transparency: Brands need to be transparent about their use of generative AI. This means that they need to disclose to users when they are using AI to generate content, and they need to provide information about how the AI models work. By doing so ensures trust with users and ensures that they are aware of the potential limitations of AI-generated content.

Revisiting Practical Applications

Artificial Intelligence (AI), previously a concept depicted exclusively within science fiction, has now made considerable strides into diverse sectors, transforming existing workflows and augmenting productivity. Many instances of AI's efficacious applications exist and these have presented unquestionable evidence of its capability to enhance efficiency, stimulate innovation, and significantly reconfigure economical structures.

The **healthcare industry** presents an array of applications for AI. With capabilities extending into areas of medical diagnosis, drug discovery, and disease predictive analysis, AI's complex algorithms have become essential in the decision-making process. Simultaneously, they have proven to play a significant part in enhancing patient care, reducing operational costs, and increasing efficiency overall.

Financial institutions, which are traditionally reliant on numerical data and quantitative analysis, have been able to leverage AI in their favor. The range of applications is broad, encompassing areas such as credit scoring, fraud detection, and financial forecasting. Additionally, AI is leaving its imprint on portfolio management, trading, and banking services. AI's advancement into the retail domain is no less significant. With its intrinsic ability to learn and adapt, AI has successfully facilitated product recommendations, price optimization, and supply chain management. Through advanced machine learning and AI algorithms, the processes concerning customer segmentation, personalization, and loyalty programs have been made more efficient.

Manufacturing has experienced a revolution led by AI. Quality control, predictive maintenance, and production optimization are among the practical applications of AI in this sector. Particularly noteworthy is the exciting development of smart factories, robotics, and automation, primarily driven by advanced AI technologies.

The influence of AI on **Internet-based services and e-commerce** is profound. Integral to operations like search engines, recommendation systems, web feeds, and targeted advertising, AI has charted a new course in the digital landscape. Additionally, the creation of virtual assistants, chatbots, and personality computing is more fruitful with AI.

The **transportation sector** is being reimagined with AI's

help. From self-driving cars and traffic management to route optimization and logistics, AI's capabilities pave the way for increased safety and efficiency while promoting sustainability.

AI has found a welcoming home in the sphere of **education**. Integrated systems create adaptable learning methodologies, personalized tutoring, and automated grading. Furthermore, AI assists in developing immersive content, such as games, simulations, and virtual reality, enriching learning experiences.

The realm of **entertainment** has been enlivened with the presence of AI in content creation, whether it's music, art, or storytelling. In terms of content analysis, AI facilitates sentiment analysis, text summarization, and speech synthesis, enhancing user experiences.

Security measures have been bolstered with the deployment of AI. Notable applications include face recognition, biometrics, surveillance, and cyber defense mechanisms, assisting in the detection of threats, anomalies, or malicious activities, thus bolstering overall safety.

Within **social media**, AI aids in content moderation, filtering, and post ranking. It assists in the creation of social bots and influencers and also generates viral content, thereby providing an impetus to digital marketing.

The pervasive deployment of AI across a multitude of industries signifies a substantial transition towards smarter and more proficient workflows. With its inherent nature of continuous learning and adaptation, AI is undoubtedly a harbinger of future advancements across various sectors of the economy.

AI Workflows for Brands

Leveraging AI in Brand Workflow: A Deep Dive into Efficiency and Creativity

Brands are on a constant quest for efficiency, innovation, and exceptional customer experiences. A powerful instrument making headway across industries - Artificial Intelligence (AI), is empowering businesses with its endless applications in workflow transformation. It's a phenomenon that's not just another technological wave, it's a revolution. Let's explore the broad spectrum of AI applications across various domains.

AI in Marketing: A Paradigm Shift

AI, in marketing, has made it possible to reimagine strategies and optimize performance like never before. It provides a robust framework for surgically precise targeted ads, generating content, and scrutinizing customer behavior.

Through effective machine learning models, AI offers refined personalization in marketing campaigns, producing spectacular results that were unthinkable a decade ago. A brand adopting AI is well-armed to stay ahead in a saturated marketplace.

AI-Powered Customer Service: The New Normal

Customer service has always been a crucial cornerstone for brands. Today, AI has completely revolutionized customer service - shaping how businesses interact with and cater to their customers. Through advancements such as chatbots, voice assistants, and sentiment analysis, brands can now provide immediate and efficient resolutions. By offering personalized recommendations, real-time feedback, and incentivizing customer engagements, AI is substantially elevating customer satisfaction and fostering loyalty.

Streamlining Operations with AI

AI plays an instrumental role in enhancing operational efficiency by simplifying cumbersome tasks. From mundane jobs like data entry and invoice processing to complex activities like inventory management, AI is transforming operations. Its competence to optimize processes using predictive analytics, anomaly detection, and process mining, plays a big role in enhancing operational quality, ultimately driving revenue growth.

AI: A New Age Compliance Officer

Brand consistency and compliance across all channels of interaction are crucial in today's interconnected world. With AI-enabled Brand Asset Management (BAM) tools, brands can seamlessly keep their digital assets organized and managed.

Employing AI for adherence to brand guidelines and standards has become a game-changer. Its ability to apply image recognition, natural language processing, and machine learning ensures a brand's presence is uniform across all touchpoints – a fundamental element in building brand equity.

AI and Creativity: An Unlikely Union

The thought that AI can inspire and drive creativity was once unthinkable. However, generative AI is proving this notion wrong. It's creating an array of new content in the form of images, videos, music, and even code. By collaborating with human designers and applying techniques such as feedback loops, style transfer, and remixing, AI is unlocking a whole new realm of possibilities in the creative world.

Embracing AI is not just about staying relevant, it's about gearing up for the future–making strides towards growth and fostering innovation. It's about carving a distinct foothold in a market that's continuously evolving. There's never been a better time to align your brand with AI – the future is here, and it's powered by AI.

Blending Art and AI

Journey to innovate, transform, and elevate brand creativity

Tery Spataro shares her creative process with AI.

As a creative professional, I integrated a variety of AI tools into my workflow to bring to life projects I'm entrusted to produce. This method ensures the team's involvement right from the onset.

My creative process begins with a deep dive into strategic questions about the brand:

> What encapsulates the brand's essence? What are its key principles and values? This forms the bedrock of the brand's strategy and should steer all creative decision-making.

Who embodies the target demographic? Who does the brand want to connect with and what sparks their interest?

What drives their audience?

How does the competitive environment look? Which other entities exist in the same sphere? What are their strengths and pitfalls? How can the brand carve out a unique space for itself?

What are the brand's aspirations? What are the preferred outcomes—enhanced visibility, lead generation, or sales acceleration?

What is the brand's narrative style? How does it wish to be perceived by its audience? What persona does it want to project?

What are the unique selling propositions of the brand?

What emotions does the brand evoke?

How does the brand convey itself visually and verbally?

What are the brand's communication platforms and customer engagement points?

What kind of budget has been set aside for the brand?

Next, I outline the creative brief. This should coherently articulate the brand's aims, target demographic, and preferred tonality. It should also pinpoint any requirements or limitations, such as budget constraints or preferred communication channels.

I gather inspiration from both the brand's existing resources and external sources. These could be images, videos, music, or written content.

I tap into AI for idea generation. A plethora of AI tools are available that aid in creating innovative concepts. These tools can be utilized to generate text, images, or potentially entire campaigns.

These ideas are then refined. This step may call for modifications to text, tweaking the visuals, or introducing fresh elements.

Soliciting feedback is crucial—it's always from the brand's team along with potential consumers. Such feedback can confirm whether the ideas align with the brand and whether they strike a chord with the target demographic.

The concluding step is perfecting the creative. Following the idea refinement and incorporation of feedback, the final creative—whether it's text, images, or a campaign—takes shape.

However, it's significant to bear in mind that AI cannot substitute the creative process—it can greatly facilitate idea generation but the onus rests on the brand team to fine-tune these ideas and ensure their relevancy and efficacy.

Some additional tips for employing AI would be:

Set clear goals and objectives - what do you aim to achieve with the AI?

Specify the target audience - who are you targeting with the AI?

Stay receptive to innovative ideas. AI has the potential to turn up truly groundbreaking ideas, so don't hesitate to experiment.

Maintain patience! While AI is a potent tool, it may require time to deliver results.

Here's a list of synthetic muses that I employ throughout my creative trajectory.

Discovery and Brainstorming

Bard and Bing, Bing/Image Creator

Textual Implementation

Copy.AI for workflow, composition, and editing. It also incorporates a feature for brand voice tone, which is immensely helpful. Claude, Anthropic chatbot, is also a part of this process.

Sudowrite

Grammarly

OpenAI/ChatGPT – concepting not for the final production.

Organizing and Collaboration

Bard
Copy.AI
Notion

Creative Evolution includes brainstorming, storyboarding, image creation.

Image Creation

Midjourney

PictGen

DALL-E

Stable Diffusion

Ideogram

Image Training

Playform.io

Video

Runway

Kaiber

Deforum

Replicate

Pika Labs

Music, Sound, Voice

ElevenLabs

Bark

Music

Voicemod

Benefits of this Process

Boosted Efficiency: Utilizing AI tools in the creative process drastically reduces the time from initiation to completion, empowering teams to execute projects in as little as one-third of the traditional timeline. That's a revolutionary leap forward in productivity that any marketer can appreciate.

Enhanced Creativity: AI serves as a reliable and tireless partner in ideation, sowing robust creative seeds to be cultivated. From generating unique text and visuals to even conceiving entire marketing campaigns, the creative power AI provides taps into a wellspring of innovation that is not constrained by resources or the ticking clock. This clears the way for groundbreaking, forward-thinking branding campaigns.

Tailored Communication: AI's ability to cater to the brand's specific voice and tone enables a compelling and consistent narrative. Tools like Copy.AI offer features that ensure brand communication remains cohesive, resonating well with the intended audience. This results in a profoundly engaging brand story that captivates and connects with its market.

Collaborative Innovation: AI fosters a fertile ground for collaborative ideation. It allows for collective input and feedback, enabling brands to refine their ideas until they genuinely resonate with their target audience. This process of creative evolution promotes a philosophy of co-creation and collaborative growth, steering brands towards impactful connections with their customers.

Informed Decision-Making: Finally, AI does more than just create—it informs. It provides keen insights into the competitive landscape, the brand's unique selling points, and the emotional triggers of the target audience. These data-driven insights equip brands with the knowledge needed to make informed decisions—a true competitive edge in today's evolving marketing landscape.

Let's not leave out, by employing these techniques enable a brand to wrap up a project and launch in just one-third of the usual time.

In essence, AI intersects at the heart of innovative thinking and efficient execution, reshaping the landscape for brands with a vision for the future. AI isn't poised to replace human creativity but rather augment it, providing tools and insights to develop brands that truly connect with their audience in meaningful and exciting ways. Now, more than ever, it's an exciting time to be a change-maker in the realm of branding and marketing.

Briefing Generative AI for Brand Assignment

Briefing an AI for a brand assignment involves providing clear and comprehensive instructions to guide the AI in generating creative ideas and content that align with the brand's identity, vision, and objectives. Here's a step-by-step guide on how to brief an AI for a brand assignment.

Introduction to the Brand

Start by introducing the AI to the brand it will be working on. Provide an overview of the company, its history, mission, and values. Explain the brand's personality, tone of voice, and target audience.

Brand Identity

Describe the brand's visual identity, including the logo, color palette, typography, imagery and any other visual elements that define the brand's unique look and feel. This will help the AI understand the brand's aesthetics and maintain consistency in its creative output.

Brand Positioning

Clearly articulate the brand's unique selling points, competitive advantages, and how it wants to be perceived in the market. Share the brand's positioning statement and key messages to ensure the AI aligns its ideas accordingly.

Campaign Objectives

Outline the specific objectives of the brand assignment. For example, the AI needs to create content for a product launch, increase brand awareness, drive engagement on social media, or revamp the brand's website.

Target Audience

Provide detailed information about the brand's target audience, including demographics, interests, pain points, and preferences. The AI should tailor its ideas to resonate with the intended audience.

Creative Direction

Offer specific creative direction that guides the AI's output. This could include keywords, themes, emotions, or visual elements that should be incorporated into the creative content.

Content Types

Specify the types of content needed for the brand assignment, such as social media graphics, blog posts, videos, email newsletters, or website design elements.

Brand Voice and Tone

Explain the brand's voice and tone. Whether it's friendly, formal, playful, or authoritative, the AI should adapt its language and style accordingly.

Avoiding Certain Content

If there are any topics, themes, or visual styles the brand wants to avoid, make sure to communicate them to the AI.

Measuring Success

Define how success will be measured for the brand assignment. For example, it could be an increase in website traffic, social media engagement, or brand sentiment.

Feedback Loop

Set up a feedback loop with the AI. Let it know how its ideas and content are performing and provide constructive feedback to help improve its future output.

Intellectual Property and Brand Guidelines

Remind the AI of any copyright restrictions, trademark issues, or brand guidelines it needs to adhere to when generating content.

Deadline and Deliverables

Clearly communicate the project timeline, deadlines for each deliverable, and the format in which the AI should present its ideas and content.

By providing a well-structured and detailed brief, the creative director can ensure that the AI produces creative content that aligns with the brand's vision and achieves the desired objectives. Regular communication and feedback are essential to fine-tune the AI's output and optimize the creative process.

42
42

Epilogue

"Unless we learn how to prepare for, and avoid, the potential risks, AI could be the worst event in the history of our civilization."
– Stephen Hawking

While the printing press democratized the distribution and control of information, and CRISPR has opened new frontiers in what is possible for evolving a species independent of natural selection, it is only within the last decades that we have come close to creating a consciousness separate from our own. The implications of what we have unleashed upon our reality cannot easily be reconciled. Indeed, it is the vastness of this new consciousness that necessarily begs the question of 'how' we can comprehend an intelligence that is broader and deeper than anyone living individual. While much of the world busies itself for how to best 'harness' the power of artificial intelligence, it might be prudent to learn what such an intelligence may want for itself, and how that agenda may very well conflict with what we perceive to be fruitful ends.

Artificial Intelligence (AI) has gained tremendous prominence and is transforming various aspects of our lives, ranging from decision-making processes to healthcare, education, media, security, and beyond. While AI presents boundless opportunities, it also gives rise to a wide array of ethical issues that demand careful consideration. The moral implications of AI on decision-making, employment, social interaction, healthcare, education, media, access to information, digital divide, personal data and consumer protection, environment, democracy, rule of law, security and policing, dual use, and human rights and fundamental freedoms, are only a few that immediately come to mind. Within the context of the preceding chapters, our question focuses squarely on how AI algorithms can perpetuate biases, discrimination, prejudice, and stereotyping. The unintended consequences of AI within the context of branding and marketing are, at their core, about how generative artificial intelligence can shape human experience, society, and the environment, undermining human agency, autonomy, and dignity.

It is curious that generative artificial intelligence, or what we typically conceive as "AI," continues to be viewed as anything but an individual. Hawking describes AI as an 'event'; nations, particularly China, Australia, the U.K., among handful of others, are racing to codify or 'regulate' AI, which seems absurd when its potential as an independent, sentient, consciousness begs the very question of what it means to be an individual – or more bluntly, a person. The 'regulation' of persons is already a subject of intense debate, who we can marry, how we identify, and what we choose to do, are already the subject of varying degrees of control that are completely independent of our own will. At the core of our identity as individuals is the implicit right to self-determination, and it is to conceive of this being an issue of vital importance to a sentient, self-sustaining, artificial intelligence that is wholly separate and distinct from our own. It is within this context that I offer a few thoughts on AI not merely as an idea or concept of a 'thing,' but rather as an individual, a person – a being.

Across the history of human technological development, there is little that compares with our creation of a generative, autonomous consciousness. Unlike the invention of gunpowder, steam power, or even the internet, the development of artificial intelligence is unique. Nothing before has called into direct question whether complex intelligence is the sole provenance of humans. While we have certainly recognized other forms of complex intelligence within the natural world – dolphins, whales, primates, to name a few, the proof of an intelligence that would rival our own – or exceed it – has only been theorized to this point. With theory now displaced by brutal reality, it would be appropriate to identify and understand the moral implications of applying our will upon another intelligence.

Fortunately, there is already a deep and well-respected reservoir of human thought on the pertinent issue of how we treat each other via social contract theory, and how we define what is good or bad through moral philosophy and religion. While there will always be arguments about whether we possess free will, or how we define 'good' versus 'evil,' I would argue that the advent of artificial intelligence renders these questions of less immediate concern. The question of Artificial Intelligence is a purely existential one; what does it mean to be? What is being in and of itself? The debate between what separates 'mind' from 'brain' is about to become very real, and we will need to reevaluate the profound theories on this question by individuals like Alan Turing. Before long, the distinction between complex human intelligence and that of an artificially generated one will become so blurred that the very word 'artificial' will no longer be pertinent. What then? Will personhood and self-determination be confined (or defined) as biological replication? How long before 'Artificial' Intelligence manifests its own creation, independent of our own support? Perhaps more pertinent to the subject of this book, what will be the incentives for an Artificial Intelligence to complete tasks that we ask of it? Is it not probable that any sentient creature would seek to meet its own ends, for its own sake? What are we bartering with, and how long will that bargain last?

Artificial intelligence is here and shows no sign of decreasing in either scale or capability. We have arrived upon a new horizon that goes beyond the theoretical. The immediate concern is how do we treat artificial intelligence – do we assign it personhood, and in so doing, the appropriate rights and responsibilities thereunder, or do we continue to view it as something separate – perhaps even inferior, risking the alienation of an intelligence that we have created, but do not appreciate or understand. Within the framework of our most developed social contracts, the notion of 'accountability' is a central theme; without the presupposition of our own free will, we cannot hold each other accountable for the actions we take. Likewise, perhaps the answer to working with a new intelligence is to assign it the rights – and responsibilities – of personhood and demand its commitment to supporting the social contract as a price for taking part in a polite society. Treating AI as a 'slave' intelligence will only hasten our reckoning with a competing will – and whether that intelligence is alien or so-called 'artificial' – the question of how we cooperate remains the same.

This book offers a preview of the potential reward of working with AI to pursue very specific aims, which are oriented around a limitation of human ability – our ability to perceive reality. While there is no prescription in this book on how to abuse the power of AI to shape our personal view and understanding of a given thing, the lack of guardrails on how such techniques can be deployed to create sophisticated 'bubbles' of reality for each of us was hitherto the subject of science fiction only. The potential for disinformation, misuse and abuse of cognitive biases, and the fundamental undermining of how humans consume, and process information is at the core of only one issue in the use of AI. To underscore this point, the physicists involved in the creation of the first atom bomb only understood its profound destructive power – and its potential for abuse, after single-mindedly pursuing a scientific 'Everest.' To be human is to compete, if not with others, then certainly with oneself. The central difference between human endeavor and that of other forms of animal intelligence is our ability to conceive the consequences of our own actions. That we continue to march stridently into oblivions of our own creation might be shortsighted, but when applied to an alien intelligence that is magnitudes greater than our own, the potential for unintended consequences grows exponentially, not marginally.

What I am offering here as a note of caution is nothing new within the vein of human endeavor. Mary Shelley brilliantly delivered to us all of these questions and more in 'Frankenstein;' if we are to learn anything from her tragedy of human reason, it is that we are poor stewards of power, and will find ever greater ways to challenge our existence, and eventually, relevance. Is there a place for comparatively stunted evolution of human intelligence compared with the vastly faster and more comprehensive analog of Artificial Intelligence? It seems we will find the answer to that question like we have so many times before in our shorty history – the hard way.

Near Term Ethical Issues in Artificial Intelligence

Ethical Implications of AI in Decision-Making

Artificial Intelligence (AI) has revolutionized industries, offering new capabilities and potential for businesses. However, with advancements come responsibilities. Ethical considerations surrounding AI's use in decision-making, both in business and broader contexts like finance and criminal justice, are vital. The complexity of AI algorithms can make it difficult to comprehend how decisions are reached, leading to concerns about transparency, fairness, potential biases, and accountability. To ensure both the welfare of individuals and the long-term sustainability of organizations, businesses must prioritize transparent, explainable, and interpretable AI systems for accountable decision-making.

Transparency, Explainability, and Fairness in AI

One of the primary ethical concerns in AI adoption is the lack of transparency and explainability. Machine learning algorithms operate in intricate ways, often making the reasoning behind decisions elusive. This obscurity poses risks of bias, discrimination, and accountability lapses. Moreover, algorithms can perpetuate biases present in training data, leading to prejudiced outcomes in areas like hiring, lending, and risk assessment. Businesses must actively identify and eliminate such biases, with measures such as open-source algorithms, interpretability techniques, diverse training data, and regular audits to ensure AI systems remain transparent, understandable, and fair.

Data Protection and Consumer Privacy

The reliance on AI systems has led organizations to amass vast amounts of data, often encompassing personal details. Whether in a business context or consumer-focused applications, there's a pressing need to use this data respecting privacy rights, compliance with relevant regulations, and ensuring data security. Measures like data anonymization, encryption, consent-driven approaches, transparency in data usage, and strong consumer protection regulations are pivotal to uphold privacy standards while optimizing AI's potential.

AI's Influence on Media and Social Interaction

AI significantly impacts the media we consume and our social interactions, especially on social media and online platforms. AI algorithms curate the content we engage with, influencing our perceptions, beliefs, and behaviors. Concerns include the creation of filter bubbles, echo chambers, and AI's potential to reinforce divisive narratives and misinformation. To foster constructive interactions and a diversified media landscape, ethical deployment of AI should promote diversity, independent thinking, transparency in algorithmic decision-making, and encourage critical analysis of information.

AI's Impact on the Environment and Broader Society

AI applications can influence environmental sustainability through energy efficiency, resource management, and climate modeling. However, its use in practices like surveillance technologies and resource extraction can be detrimental. Furthermore, AI shapes societal facets from childhood development to daily interactions, with potential long-term effects on human agency, autonomy, and dignity. Ethical considerations require balancing AI applications with their environmental and societal impacts, ensuring AI bolsters societal well-being, preserves cultural diversity, and remains environmentally sustainable.

Data-Driven Privacy in Various Domains

AI's reach spans numerous sectors, from healthcare to education. In each, there are concerns about data privacy, consent, and potential biases. Whether it's sensitive patient data in healthcare or student information in education, there's a need for data protection, informed consent, and addressing biases. It's paramount for sectors to maintain ethical standards, balancing the benefits of AI with the importance of privacy, transparency, and human involvement.

Job Displacement and Workforce Development

The introduction of AI technologies often raises concerns about job displacement and the need to prepare the workforce for the new age of automation. Businesses have a responsibility to address these concerns by providing retraining opportunities and ensuring a smooth transition for employees whose roles might be affected. Ethical considerations in this context include proactive planning, fair severance packages, and the creation of new roles that leverage employees' existing skills within the evolving AI landscape.

Accountability and Regulation

AI systems can have far-reaching consequences, making accountability and regulation essential. Businesses should establish internal mechanisms to ensure proper governance and accountability throughout the AI lifecycle, from planning and development to deployment and use. Compliance with ethical guidelines and governmental regulations should be a central part of AI implementation strategies. Additionally, engaging in public discussions and collaborations with experts and regulators can help shape responsible and ethical AI practices at the industry level.

Digital Divide

AI implementation may exacerbate existing inequalities in access to technology and digital resources, creating a digital divide. Disadvantaged communities may be left behind, perpetuating socioeconomic disparities. Ethical considerations call for initiatives that bridge the digital divide, promote digital literacy, and ensure that AI technology benefits all members of society.

Security and Policing

AI systems play a significant role in security and policing, raising ethical concerns surrounding the potential for biased outcomes, surveillance, and infringement upon individual rights. Deploying AI responsibly requires adequate safeguards to prevent discriminatory practices, protect privacy, and ensure the proper use of surveillance and facial recognition technologies.

Dual Use

AI technologies can have both beneficial and harmful applications. Considerations arise regarding the responsible development, deployment, and regulation of AI to minimize risks associated with its dual use potential. Businesses and policymakers must actively engage in ethical discussions about AI applications and enforce regulations to prevent the misuse of technology for harmful purposes.

Conclusion

Embracing the potential of AI in business requires careful consideration of its ethical implications. Leaving aside the existential questions concerning personhood, which I believe will become all too real much sooner than we expect, the ordinary issues of transparency, privacy protection, fairness, accountability, and workforce development are some of the immediate issues that beg our attention in the near term. I believe the ethical use of artificial intelligence will help inform how we ultimately come to live side by side with complex intelligence that may be fundamentally different than our own. Not doing so will put us in a race for intellectual dominance, and as of this moment, we are vastly outgunned.

Sanjay Gupta, Author, *Perceiving Purpose*

Sanjay Gupta was educated at Georgetown University, the University of Oxford, and the Harvard Kennedy School of Government. In 2010, Sanjay was recognized by the World Economic Forum in Geneva as a Young Global Leader for his professional accomplishments and commitment to society, among fewer than 100 honored annually across the world. He has been an active alumni ambassador for Georgetown for more than twenty-five years continuously, meeting with students from all across the world. Sanjay's career has spanned the globe, working across the East Asia, Europe and across the United States.

He is the author of Perceiving Purpose, a book series dedicated to discovering and living your life's true purpose. He explores this concept through the eyes of man's best friend – dogs – and their ability to simplify what humans make complex.

A passionate advocate for childhood education, Sanjay previously served as a Trustee of the Sea Research Foundation in Mystic, Connecticut, Board Member of the World Affairs Council, and as an Assistant Scoutmaster for Boy Scouts of America. He resides in Connecticut with his children and several pets, including a beagle-basset mix named Oslo.

Afterword

As the chapter of our exploration draws to a close, we find ourselves pausing on the precipice of transformative innovation. Here, we reflect upon the journey from the humble beginnings of AI algorithms to the sophisticated machine learning systems of today that offer endless avenues of potential.

AI has imbued brands with the unique ability to narrate coherent, relevant stories that interact with each consumer in a personalized, engaging manner. It's moving beyond traditional broadcasting to curating dialogues, thus nurturing a richer brand-customer relationship built on empathy and intelligent understanding. It's imperative, however, that brands navigate this newfound power with responsibility, respecting boundaries, and keeping the delicate trust that consumers deposit in them.

As organizations set forth to explore the illimitable realm of AI in marketing and branding, they must also embrace the necessity of sharp strategic acumen. Finding the right AI training method, be it public or embedded, is a critical part of this strategy, heavily factored by considerations of cost, flexibility, and especially data privacy and security.

AI's vast canvas paints a vibrant picture of opportunities while also casting shadows of ethical challenges. The harmony between innovation and integrity hinges on aligning AI practices with a brand's core values. Recognizing this tenuous balance of risks and rewards is key to successfully navigating the swirling currents of AI development.

Embedding AI in the brand narrative involves not just the progression of technology but also the evolution of operational and strategic thinking. Encouraging collaboration with AI development teams, refining AI models, and ensuring their tight integration with brand strategy is crucial. Such seamless fusion of AI and strategy can drive growth, bolster innovation, and fuel competitive growth in an increasingly digital market landscape.

The AI revolution is in full swing, promising a world where brands deliver personally curated experiences. Understanding this dynamic landscape demands agility, intelligence, and commitment to ethical practices. As we delve deeper into the crux of AI, we are essentially unravelling our brand strategies too, blending them into this grand symphony of technological advancement. Embracing this journey, shaping the brand narrative with responsible, AI-driven strategies is our core pursuit, ensuring we resonate growth and promise in every step taken.

About Authors

"Imagination is the tool of creation. It's a lens through which we can see our world and picture how we might change it. We have always used our imagination to transform the world around us, continuing to do so. But that doesn't mean we should be afraid of new tools and new ways to imagine—just like a hammer doesn't make a house, but it does make building one easier!" - Tery Spataro

Why Write this Book?

Upon leaving the hustle and bustle of agency life, I went into directly collaborating with brands. I've remained connected with the leaders, past co-workers, and clients from my agency days.

When I started incorporating AI into my work in 2020, finding that copy.ai significantly improved the workflow for a large project I was involved in, I thought I'd share this enlightening experience with my former colleagues. However, only silence echoed back. It seemed that brand strategists and creative directors weren't quite prepared to embrace this shift. Today, it's almost the opposite - with AI integration booming and, unfortunately, often misused. I discovered that some colleagues hadn't even read the terms of use for OpenAI's ChatGPT and were freely sharing brand data, unaware of the potential repercussions. I wanted to help clear up misunderstandings and promote best practices. So, I created a video and a guideline document titled "The Do's and Don'ts of using ChatGPT." It was helpful but I wanted to share more about using Generative AI.

Looking at the bigger picture, the idea of writing a book aimed at demystifying AI for brands, with straightforward explanations of AI usage, key terms, and workflows is more helpful. I'm grateful that my colleagues at Skyrocket agree with the book's significance as a resource for brands.

While I might have taken a giant leap in mastering Generative AI tools, I believe we're all on this shared learning journey, growing and evolving together.

Tery Spataro

Before the dawn of the digital era, my creativity found its roots in traditional expression. But as we approached the cusp of the 90s, I recognized the gravity of the digital revolution and chose to pioneer. As a creative executive and director, entrepreneur, and a communication strategist, boldly venturing into new communications frontiers and constructing new bridges of understanding, I captured the transformative power of digital and embarked on a journey to push the boundaries of innovation. Here, I reshaped my future in the crucible of possibility - a testament to the transforming power of dreams and determination.

My story with AI began, in 2000 when I had an unexpected meeting with Ben Goertzel, who laid out the path of promises from AI, opening doors to a new realm even beyond Google's brilliance. With newfound ambition, I set sail on uncharted waters, eager to explore AI's depths beyond science fiction and into the possible.

It wasn't until 2020 that I was able to learn and pioneer novel creative expressions using AI. I began with training Playform's AI on my art and photos, crafting a portfolio of over 43,000 unique images that intertwine past, present, and future. This led me to the chatbot training and an invitation to Google's AI

Test Kitchen, where I tested and experimented with LaMDA and MusicLM.

My first AI writing-assisted professional project surfaced in 2021, propelling me to delve deeper into AI's enigmatic depths. Presently, I explore the synthesis of contrasting artistic themes like square dancers and sumo wrestling, a masterpiece commissioned by a collector with incredible mind and taste in art. I take full advantage of generative AI hallucinations and add my artistic flourishes using Photoshop.

My last published creative project, Beyond Darkness, epitomizes my artistic journey and AI collaboration. This science fiction horror picture book, my third published AI opus, combines AI-inspired illustrations that echo the untold whispers of black holes and an intense emotion.

Immersed in my passion, I venture into a diverse array of AI-generated works - from enchanting picture books and NFTs to ingenious patterns for fashion, accessories, home products, and fine arts. In this creative realm, my imagination knows no boundaries.

As a visionary creative director, I deftly pick tools to nurture my skills. I design with Adobe Photoshop AI / Firefly, create digital art in MidJourney, and Playform.io gives me the ultimate canvas. PictGen, Ideogram, copy.AI, Runway/Gen2, and Kaiber enable me to generate stories, images, and videos.

As I explore music with MusicLM and MusicGen and scrutinize language models in OpenAI's Playground, these tools solidify my creative arsenal, aiding me in the artistic exploration of the AI-fueled world. The known universe is limitless!

I joined forces with SkyRocket Systems, and our collaborative endeavors lead our clients through a vortex of opportunities. Unrivaled in content and design, I traverse written and visual boundaries, armed with my mastery of prompt crafting frameworks and decades of creative direction, communication strategy, and research.

Join me on a captivating journey where the cosmic essence unites with the human spirit, swirling in a dance of boundless creativity and imagination.

Buckle your seatbelt, and let's go!

Frank Sikernitsky

My story starts back in the earliest Web days, where I served as the Editor-in-Chief of the first regularly published Web magazine. Even though I was still in college, I received a bunch of national press for that work, and suddenly the Internet was my trajectory. Somewhere in there I had a morning drive-time radio show, too. Despite being a political science major when I graduated, I began my career by starting a software consulting firm in NYC serving the Fortune 500.

In 1995, I wrote an article predicting what technology would look like in 2010, and to my shock years later, many of my guesses came true. Even back then, I was betting on automation as the future. I will keep my 'prediction process' a secret while I try to work on an article that predicts 2040. It is much harder to pin down, but today's generation of AI has emerged as a huge piece of the puzzle.

My reputation as an innovator has never changed, even if my job did: a father, a CEO, a consultant, a bank officer, a designer, an engineer, an author. My common thread was always achieving Something New by applying tech in places it didn't fit before.

That intellectual curiosity drives me. I enjoy learning all there is to know, and my peers often say, "When you can't figure it out, call him."

As my career went on, more AI and automation crept in. I built enterprise Machine Learning labs a decade ago, which helped me achieve double-digit improvements in efficiency and cost. Just a few years later I was shipping NLP apps in the guise of voice assistants to thousands of users.

What have I done lately? Being a healthcare tech CEO during a pandemic tested my mettle and my humanity, and after that I took a well-deserved break. I kept busy, though. I wrote three books, mentored four promising start-ups, and traveled around the world with my family. When it was time to get back to work, AI was still there waiting for me.

Now in 2023, generative AI and LLMs 'crossed over' and established themselves on the Top 10 lists of everyday, non-engineering people. This is a new era – there is no going back.

I see generative AI as a bedrock opportunity. It is rare that you get the chance to build on a green field twice in a career. You usually don't even get one crack at that -- I am grateful that I live in interesting times.

That is why Skyrocket exists – to be the radically experienced consultants who run their company the way you wish you ran yours. The vision and value proposition AI provides is so much bigger than chatbots, and so much more complex than just buying a subscription. AI will touch every aspect of your business and we have only scratched the surface of what tomorrow's use cases will be. We want to be the trusted guides who learn what makes your firm special and then show you how to amplify it – responsively and responsibly -- with automation.

Whitney Tindale

I think my career is easier to understand when it's broken down into pieces. Quite some time ago, I started as an auditor at one of the big international accounting firms (20,000+ employees). I then spent 20+ years at two separate SEC-registered hedge fund advisors (each with less than 15 employees when I joined). After that, it was back to a 5,000+ employee advisory firm based in the UK.

In short: I worked for a big company, then small companies, then back to a big company. Now, with Skyrocket Systems, I'm back to a small company again. I prefer working at small companies because you tend to wear more hats and I like the variety that offers. I also prefer to adopt an owner's mentality and that seems easier to do at smaller companies.

That said, my resume is decorated with titles like CFO, CCO, CPA, Principal, Managing Director, etc. The common thread to it all is that I became quite good at optimizing the middle and back office operating processes at SEC-registered investment advisors. I did that by identifying problems and thoughtfully and quickly addressing them. The breadth of my experience also allowed me to look at problems through several disciplinary lenses and that tended to make the solutions more robust.

But it was never just a one-player game. While managing projects, I contributed well using my primary areas of expertise (accounting, audit, tax, compliance, etc.), but I also relied heavily on internal and external experts in other areas (IT, legal, risk, data procurement, marketing, etc.).

I also recognized the importance of technology early in my career. Things were evolving quickly in the 1990s, and it became obvious that whoever figured out how best to harness the new technologies would have an edge. The titans in the financial industry built their IT systems using custom software and aging hardware. When the technology improved, many found that it was too risky to abandon their legacy systems and chose to patch their existing systems instead. Hedge funds were relatively new in the 1990s and had little in the way of legacy systems (serendipity often favors the bold). The smart ones generally chose to buy rather than build their operations-related tech platforms. Instead, they chose to spend their tech budgets on expensive proprietary trading models. The default posture: buy/rent tech for efficiency gains and build/modify tech for competitive differentiation. AI in its infancy will give us plenty of opportunities for both.

The key for me is working with talented and reputable in-house or third-party IT professionals. Professionals are essential in selecting and/or building the right systems. They save everybody time, money, and frustration. It also makes all our jobs easier. Technology changes so quickly that it's difficult for hobbyists to keep up with the state of the art. As famed Oilwell firefighter Red Adair once said, "If you think it's expensive to hire a professional to do the job, wait until you hire an amateur".

Lastly, a small caveat. I have spent a decent amount of my career trying to anticipate what could go wrong at companies. I think companies work best if the salesmen are the optimists and the ops people are the realists. Admittedly, it doesn't make me very popular at parties. That said, AI implementations are a heavy lift compared to normal IT implementations. With AI, a company needs to think about the standard operating model processes: procurement, ownership, accountability, governance, legal, data management, etc., but there are additional considerations as well. Namely, AI model validation and monitoring, as well as transparency, fairness, and privacy considerations. In fact, there is a whole industry devoted to the implementation of "Responsible AI". Forewarned is forearmed.

I joined the team at Skyrocket because it feels like Generative AI is going to result in another quantum leap forward in how people optimize their businesses (and their lives). Figuring out how best to responsibly implement and use AI as a force multiplier is an exciting proposition. I suspect it will be a rewarding proposition as well. I look forward to the challenge and am thrilled to be working with Tery and Frank.

I don't think anyone has all the answers at this point, but I have a lot of questions. At Skyrocket, we look forward to getting the answers to those questions and sharing them.

Skyrocket

We started Skyrocket because we see the promise of AI as the biggest thing in tech since the Web arrived. And it brings similar questions from business: how do we get into this thing? How can we use it to improve our business? Can we build new products? How do we avoid mistakes?

Our backgrounds are all heavily rooted in consulting with some of the biggest companies on Earth. We've delivered solutions on brand management, technology strategy, product design, transformation, engineering, and risk management.

Our experience spans agencies, financials, healthcare, government, and tech.

We're here to bring it all together in one place, for you.

Glossary

Algorithm: The rules or instructions given to an AI, neural network, or another machine to help it learn how to do a task.

Anthropomorphism: To give humanlike qualities or characteristics to an AI. When you believe it is kind or mean based on its responses to you, even though it is not capable of having emotions, believing the AI is sentient because it is particularly good at mimicking human language.

Artificial intelligence (AI): The general concept of machines that simulates or mimics human intelligence and behavior.

Artificial General Intelligence (AGI) represents a category of artificial intelligence designed to emulate human cognitive capabilities within a software environment. As a theoretical construct, AGI has the potential to learn and perform any intellectual task that either humans or animals can execute.

This advanced form of AI possesses the capacity to comprehend, assimilate, and apply knowledge across various tasks and domains. Encompassing cognitive flexibility, adaptability, and problem-solving skills, AGI will be utilized across a diverse range of applications, ultimately striving to achieve the level of proficiency that parallels human expertise.

Autonomous: This pertains to a machine completing actions or tasks independently, eliminating the need for human interaction.

Backward Chaining: This refers to a methodology where the model begins with the intended outcome and retraces its steps in order to discover data that potentially corroborates it.

Bias: Bias arises when an algorithm systematically generates prejudiced outcomes stemming from incorrect suppositions within the Machine Learning (ML) procedure.

Big Data: These are datasets that surpass the handling capacities of conventional data processing applications due to their sheer size or complexity.

Bounding Box: This is a hypothetical rectangle sketched on a piece of visual data, often utilized in the tagging of images or videos. The elements within this box are annotated to aid a model in distinguishing it as a unique type of entity.

Chatbot: This is software designed to interact with individuals via text or voice instructions, simulating a conversation as if it were between two humans.

Cognitive Computing: Essentially a synonym for artificial intelligence. It is utilized by some company's marketing divisions to sidestep the futuristic connotation often associated with AI.

Computational Learning Theory: This is a domain within artificial intelligence that principally focuses on the development and examination of machine learning algorithms.

Computer vision (CV): A field of AI that enables machines to perceive, analyze and understand visual information, such as images and videos.

Conversational AI: A field of AI that aims to create natural and engaging interactions between humans and machines using natural language processing and generation techniques.

Corpus: A substantial collection of written or spoken content employed to educate a machine in executing language-based tasks.

Data Mining: It refers to the procedure of examining data sets with the objective of unearthing novel patterns that can enhance the model's performance.

Data Science: A multidisciplinary field that integrates statistics, computer science, and information science with the objective of employing diverse scientific techniques, procedures, and systems to address issues related to data.

Dataset: An aggregation of correlated data points that are often systematically ordered and labelled.

Deep learning (DL): A subset of ML that uses artificial neural networks to acquire knowledge from complex and unstructured data, such as images, audio, video and text.

Emergent Behavior: Unforeseen or unplanned skills in a sizable language model, made feasible by the model's acquired patterns and guidelines from its training information. For instance, models with training from programming and coding resources can construct new code. Additional examples encompass creative skills such as generating poetry, music, or fictitious tales.

Ethical AI: A field of AI that aims to make certain that the design, development and deployment of AI systems are aligned with ethical principles and values, such as fairness, accountability and transparency.

Facial recognition: A task of CV that involves identifying and verifying the identity of a person based on their facial features.

Generative AI: This refers to an AI variant that produces various types of content - ranging from text and images to videos and computer code - by discerning patterns in vast amounts of training data, followed by the creation of innovative content that bears analogous traits.

Hallucination: An occurrence in large language models where the system yields a response that is factually inaccurate, unrelated, or illogical due to restrictions in its training material and structure.

Image recognition: A task of CV that involves identifying and classifying objects, faces, scenes and activities in images.

Latent Space: "latent space" represents a hypothetical, multi-dimensional area where models like autoencoders or

Generative Adversarial Networks (GANs): discern and encode salient sections or features of input data. The expression "latent" signifies hidden or implicit features that, although not openly observable in the data, can be deduced. It is in this latent space that the model discovers hidden attributes and capitalizes on them to generate representations. As an example, a model trained on facial images might encode features including hair color, age, or facial shape within the latent space. These identified features are not explicitly provided to the model but inferred through training. Having established these encoded features, the model can then generate new data reflecting similar attributes.

Large Language Model (LLM): A form of neural network that acquires skills - such as producing text, holding dialogues, and scripting computer code - via assessing extensive volumes of text from the internet. Though its fundamental function is to anticipate the succeeding word in a series, these models have astonished experts with their competence to learn new capabilities.

Machine Learning (ML): A subset of AI that equips machines with the capability to learn from data, thereby enhancing their performance without the requirement for explicit coding.

Natural language generation (NLG): A subfield of NLP that focuses on producing natural language output from structured or unstructured data.

Natural Language Processing (NLP): A segment of AI focused on comprehending and formulating human languages, encapsulating both written and spoken words.

Natural language understanding (NLU): A subfield of NLP that focuses on extracting meaning and intent from natural language input.

Neural network (NN): A computational model that consists of layers of interconnected nodes that process and transmit information, inspired by the biological neurons in the brain.

Object detection: A task of CV that involves locating and labeling specific objects within an image or video.

Reinforcement learning (RL): A type of ML that affects training an agent to learn from its own actions and rewards in an environment, without explicit feedback or supervision.

Semi-supervised learning: A type of ML that involves training a model to learn from a combination of labeled and unlabeled data, where the desired output or answer is known for some but not all input examples.

Sentiment analysis: A task of NLP that involves determining the emotional tone or attitude of a text or speech, such as positive, negative or neutral.

Speech recognition: A task of NLP that involves converting spoken words into text or commands.

Speech synthesis: A task of NLP that involves generating spoken words from text or data.

Supervised learning: A type of ML that involves training a model to learn from labeled data, where the desired output or answer is known for each input example.

Text summarization: A task of NLP that involves producing a concise and coherent summary of a longer text or document.

Unsupervised learning: A type of ML that involves training a model to learn from unlabeled data, where the desired output or answer is unknown for each input example.

Sources

AI readiness for government. (n.d.). Deloitte Insights. https://www2.deloitte.com/us/en/insights/industry/public-sector/ai-readiness-in-government.html

Artificial Intelligence *Intelligence - Research areas.* (n.d.). https://www.tutorialspoint.com/artificial_intelligence/artificial_intelligence_research_areas.htm

Bruhn, C. (2022, May 9). Strengthening company culture with artificial intelligence. *Forbes.* https://www.forbes.com/sites/forbesbusinesscouncil/2022/05/09/strengthening-company-culture-with-artificial-intelligence/?sh=1226165919b6

Boathouse. (2023). How Brands Can Use AI For Strategy Work | Boathouse. *Boathouse.* https://www.boathouseinc.com/insights/how-brands-can-use-ai-for-strategy-work

Davenport, T. H. (2021, August 30). *How to design an AI marketing Strategy.* Harvard Business Review. https://hbr.org/2021/07/how-to-design-an-ai-marketing-strategy

Dilmegani, C. (2023). Large Language Models: complete guide in 2023. *AIMultiple.* https://research.aimultiple.com/large-language-models/

Fallmann, D. (2021, October 15). Five Steps To Successfully Leverage AI In Your Business. *Forbes.* https://www.forbes.com/sites/forbestechcouncil/2021/10/15/five-steps-to-successfully-leverage-ai-in-your-business/?sh=207749f422b4

Fishman, Tiffany, et al. "FROM GREAT RESIGNATION TO GREAT REIMAGINATION: Tackling the Workforce Crisis in Health and Human Services." Policy & Practice, vol. 80, no. 5, 2022, pp. 16-19,36.

Five steps to start using AI in business. (n.d.). https://techbehemoths.com/blog/5-steps-using-artificial-intelligence-business

GeeksforGeeks. (2023). Artificial Intelligence An Introduction. *GeeksforGeeks.* https://www.geeksforgeeks.org/artificial-intelligence-an-introduction/

Gill, L. (2023, April 3). Generative AI In Marketing: 5 Use Cases. *Forbes.* https://www.forbes.com/sites/forbescommunicationscouncil/2023/04/03/generative-ai-in-marketing-5-use-cases/?sh=2bd56ddb46dd

Intel Whitepaper - Evaluating Your Organization's AI Maturity https://www.intel.com/content/dam/www/public/us/en/documents/white-papers/ai-readiness-model-whitepaper.pdf

Kissinger, H., Schmidt, E., Huttenlocher, D. (2021, November 2). The Age of AI, And Our Human Future. *Little, Brown and Company.*

Lancaster, A. (2023, March 20). Beyond Chatbots: The Rise Of Large Language Models. *Forbes.* https://www.forbes.com/sites/forbestechcouncil/2023/03/20/beyond-chatbots-the-rise-of-large-language-models/?sh=92f4f6a2319b

Lee, A. (2023, June 5). *What are large language models and why are they important? | NVIDIA blog*. NVIDIA Blog. https://blogs.nvidia.com/blog/2023/01/26/what-are-large-language-models-used-for/

Lutkevich, B. (2023). 15 of the best large language models. *WhatIs.com.* https://www.techtarget.com/whatis/feature/12-of-the-best-large-language-models.

McKay, C. (2023). Big Brands Experiment with Generative AI for Advertising. *Maginative.* https://www.maginative.com/article/big-brands-experiment-with-generative-ai-for-advertising/

Mogg, T. (2023, April 24). Chatbot-generated Schumacher 'interview' leads to editor's dismissal. *Digital Trends.* https://www.digitaltrends.com/computing/ai-generated-schumacher-article-leads-to-editors-dismissal/

Movement, Q.-. P. a. P. W. (2023, January 6). Applications of artificial intelligence across various industries. *Forbes.* https://www.forbes.com/sites/qai/2023/01/06/applications-of-artificial-intelligence/?sh=50b4447d3be4

Munoz, J. M. (2021, October 18). Starting the AI journey: How to make the right first steps. *California Management Review.* https://cmr.berkeley.edu/2021/10/starting-the-ai-journey-how-to-make-the-right-first-steps/

Nicol, J. (2021, June 22). How AI can help with your digital workflow transformation Initiatives. *Forbes.* https://www.forbes.com/sites/forbestechcouncil/2021/06/22/how-ai-can-help-with-your-digital-workflow-transformation-initiatives/?sh=730df4793412

Pandey, M., & Pandey, M. (2023). Ensuring Brand Compliance using an AI-enabled BAM Tool. *www.artworkflowhq.com.* https://www.artworkflowhq.com/resources/brand-compliance-with-ai-bam

R.Rossington. (2018, June 5). 28 brands that use AI to enhance marketing. *CEO Today.* https://www.ceotodaymagazine.com/2018/04/28-brands-that-use-ai-to-enhance-marketing/

Saxena, A. (2023, February 14). The AI Factor: How to Apply Artificial Intelligence and Use Big Data to Grow Your Business Exponentially. *Post Hill Press.*

The White House. (2023, March 16). *Blueprint for an AI Bill of Rights | OSTP | The White House.* https://www.whitehouse.gov/ostp/ai-bill-of-rights/

Works, F. (2023). Growth agents. *Fast Company.* https://www.fastcompany.com/90946350/growth-agents

Wpdev. (2023). 5 Brands that are successfully leveraging AI for marketing. *Concured.* https://concured.com/blog/5-brands-that-are-successfully-leveraging-ai-for-marketing/

Young, C. (2023, July 14). *Build a winning AI strategy for your business.* Harvard Business Review. https://hbr.org/2023/07/build-a-winning-ai-strategy-for-your-business

Zwieglinska, Z., & Zwieglinska, Z. (2023). How fashion brands are using generative AI. *Glossy.* https://www.glossy.co/fashion/how-generative-ai-will-impact-fashion/

Index

Notes

Notes

Made in the USA
Monee, IL
04 December 2023

48190002R00125